GRAND CANYON ECSTASY

GRAND CANYON ECSTASY

The Psyche of Water and Stone

Dennis L. Outwater, Ph.D.

Protean Press
21 Broadway, Suite 5
Rockport, MA 01966

www.ProteanPress.com

Library of Congress Control Number: 2022918637

ISBN 978-0-9913520-9-8

First Edition 2023

Manufactured in the United States of America

Credits
Book produced by Open Book Systems, Inc. Text and cover design by Janis Owens. This book was typeset in Adobe Arno and Futura by Janis Owens.

Cover photo, chapter opener photos: printed with permission of photographer, Gary Ladd. All rights reserved.
Cover photo: Near "Duck on a Rock" viewpoint which is Southeast of Shoshone Point along the South Rim's Desert View Drive. In the distance is Vishnu Temple.

Map insert: printed with permission of cartographer, Tom Jonas. All rights reserved.

DEDICATION

I dedicate this book to my wife, Donna Outwater, who made it possible for me to find the time not only to take my solo hikes in the Grand Canyon, but also to keep the "common touch" of family, house, and garden, in balance with my reading and writing. I am indebted to her for a wonderful family and for her consistent patience and encouragement with the writing of this book. I also dedicate this book to my children, Alex and Jessica, and their families Meredith, Haley, Evan; and Bernard, Ella, and Cole, with love, always.

ACKNOWLEDGMENTS

Thanks to Paul Tillich, philosopher and theologian, who helped me obtain a full scholarship to the University of Chicago Divinity School to pursue my Masters and Ph.D. in philosophy.

Thanks to Mircea Eliade, the famous history of religion scholar, from whom I gained immeasurable knowledge, and who then gave me my written essay test for the Ph.D.

Thanks to James Hillman, whose books and scholarship educated me about the philosophical transition from childhood to adulthood.

Thanks to Wayne Ranney, the Grand Canyon geologist, and Kim Crumbo of the Wildlife Council, for their discussions about the canyon.

Thanks to Bryan Wisher, who helped me out of a difficult situation. He is a supreme example of what it means to be a Ranger in a National Park.

EDITORIAL ACKNOWLEDGMENTS

A big thank you to Laura Fillmore Evans and Marina Evans at Open Book Systems, Inc., for their willingness to read the first draft, and for their patience and expertise while taking me through the publishing process, beginning to end.

Thank you to Jennifer Bennett of JBM Words who provided a substantive edit of the manuscript, with a careful eye for words, and without compromising the author's thoughts and ideas.

Thank you to Janis Owens, book designer, who provided her artistic eye and experience in book design and photograph placement in the finished book.

Thanks to Tom Jonas in Phoenix, AZ, professional cartographer, who produced a detailed map of the Grand Canyon's trails, creeks, and points of interest in my solo hiking trips.

Thanks to Gary Ladd, a seasoned Grand Canyon photographer, who kindly shared the cover and chapter opener photos which capture the sky, the rock and the sun of the Grand Canyon landscape.

The Canyon still grips its travelers in mysticism. No one is cynical or matter-of-fact about the Grand Canyon. It is perhaps the world's greatest natural wonder. [...] The Canyon becomes a mind-altering drug, the canyoneer an addict.

—Bill Beer, *We Swam the Grand Canyon*
(15 Minute Press, Third Edition, 2008)

Nothing at all would help me to understand more clearly, in any intellectual sense, how all the scattered and disparate strands of life weave together, interlocking. But I had moved closer to the pulse of life. I had heard a new counterpoint to the unique basic rhythm of the universe. And in it I recognized the common grain that ran through everything I knew existed, including me.

—Colin Fletcher, *The Man Who Walked Through Time* (Alfred A. Knopf, 1967)

The shaman is the great specialist in the human soul; he alone "sees" it, for he knows its "form" and its "destiny."

—Mircea Eliade,
Shamanism: Archaic Techniques of Ecstasy
(Bollingen Foundation, Pantheon Books, 1964))

Surely joy is the condition of life.

—Henry David Thoreau, *Natural History of Massachusetts* (1842)

National Park designation alone does not assure the land is protected from the increasing pressure for development, nor does it require the agency to protect the visitor's "wilderness experience." Wilderness designation does. Wilderness is a "[...] land retaining its primeval character and influence [...] with the imprint of man substantially unnoticeable." Not only are non-conforming developments and practices prohibited, but where recreational use is appropriate, wilderness must provide for "outstanding opportunities for solitude or a primitive and unconfined type of recreation." The Wilderness Act mandates consideration for experiential quality.

—Kim Crumbo,
"Wilderness Management at Grand Canyon: Waiting for Godot?"
(*International Journal of Wilderness* 2(1):19-23, 1996)

I love the Grand Canyon! For me there is no more powerful place on this earth than this huge chasm of stone and light. [...] I have come of age as a human being in the depths of its salubrious embrace. In a very real way I am a child of the Grand Canyon.

— Wayne Ranney,
Carving Grand Canyon: Evidence, Theories, and Mystery
(Grand Canyon Association, 2005)

SOLO HIKING IN THE GRAND CANYON

This book does not encourage solo backpacking in the Grand Canyon unless the hiker who is considering such a thing follows reasonable and essential plans, as implied in Michael Ghiglieri and Thomas Myers's *Over the Edge: Death in the Grand Canyon* (Puma Press, Flagstaff, 2001). The book's Table 1-B is entitled "Accidental Lethal Falls While Hiking or Orienteering within Grand Canyon," and it lists forty-eight people. However, there is no data about how many, if any, **solo backpackers** have lost their lives.

Of the forty-eight only one fits the type of solo backpacker that I am encouraging—in terms of season and choice of trails. That one person was Thomas Velzy, eighteen years of age, who fell from the South Kaibab Trail 1½ miles in, with no witnesses to see his fall. His youthful age probably encouraged him to leave the trail and go to the edge of a cliff, where he fell 100ft. I took my solo trips in the Grand Canyon in my early 50s and I never walked to the edge of a cliff. Velzy's fall was at the end of September, when the canyon is very warm. More than half of my solo backpacking trips started down the South Kaibab Trail, but Velzy also was a **hiker** rather than a **solo backpacker**.

Solo backpackers do not force themselves as hikers often do, and they hike only for part of a day—a hard rule of mine—usually from early light to noon. Solo backpackers go for solitude, rather than to conquer a piece of the Grand Canyon, which is often the goal of the solo hiker. Colin Fletcher (1922–2007) was a solo hiker, but a mature man with many years of hiking under his famous belt.

Here are my rules, stated at the beginning of the book because I do not want any solo backpacker to think that a solo trip is either easy or too dangerous. It is not dangerous if you do as I did, and it is essential for those looking for ecstasy, or at least a "deep-nature-absorption" experience, to:

1. Go in March, if you can, and never in summer or early fall.
2. Go legally, with a permit, and follow exactly your itinerary.
3. Go in the Corridor if you want a quality experience, between Hermit Creek Campground and Cottonwood Campground on the edge of Horseshoe Mesa. There, you will find solitude, especially in March, but also a few people in case you get into trouble.
4. Use the Tonto Trail, either east or west, and cache your food and water on the way out to the east or west. On the return, reclaim your caches as you hike towards one of the two maintained trails—Bright Angel Trail or South Kaibab Trail—thereby reducing your overall pack weight.
5. Prepare for your trip with lots of exercise, especially of the legs.
6. Don't look at the scenery when walking, and on the few exposures, use my discussed procedures for maximum exposure walking (if you must) while wearing a pack.
7. Find a good sporting goods store for help with your needed materials, especially your backpack, tent, and sleeping bag, plus stove and water pump, as well as cooking pot and water canteens. The best is the lightest and simplest, and before getting on the trail, practice with a full pack at home and then on the Grand Canyon rim (high elevation) before the descent.
8. Check out the two maintained trails because mules are damaging them, especially at the top of Bright Angel Trail and on the lower end of South Kaibab Trail before the Tonto Trail.

9. On arrival at the Grand Canyon, spend a day walking the rim to get used to the elevation. Set out on the second day and only if the weather forecast is good.

10. Get a very early start, using two poles and crampons when necessary. Always walk on the inside of the trail.

11. If possible, familiarize yourself with your chosen trail with just a small day pack, trail mix, and water before starting your solo backpacking trip. Trail acquaintance is very useful.

12. Perhaps the most important rule: Solo backpackers are not trekkers, so plan on hiking only a few hours and taking off the afternoon and sunset to have stone and creek time, eating dinner before dark. Get to sleep in your tent early so that you can wake at dawn (about 4 am) and be on the trail before the sun is heating it up. Use both poles, and if you walk on sunlit earth in the early morning, watch out for rattlesnakes. Let them strike your poles, not your legs. When you come to a new site, use your poles to check out every rock close to your campsite by hitting the stones and listening for a snakes' rattle. I have never found a rattlesnake, but always use my poles just to be sure they're not there.

13. Watch out for bats in Salt Canyon, or any slot or semi-slot canyons. They will defend their water pools. God knows what their bite contains!

Prepare fully and relish the solitude. More than one person constitutes a "group site," so you don't have to share your site if you are looking for solitude. A quality experience requires lots of solitude, at least three or four days of it. Then, maybe: ecstasy. It happened to me, so why not you? You will never forget it. The Grand Canyon was formed by water on stone, so make the descent, discover true solitude, and return with a part of "the psyche of water and stone." A Grand Canyon ecstasy will transform your life.

CONTENTS

PREFACE

CHAPTER 1

CREMATION IN Z FLAT

Side Canyons
1. Descent into Muddy Waters
2. The Miracle Cave Rock
3. The First Shelter
4. Raven Wash
5. Grapevine's Stone Time
6. Scout Leader Dynamics
7. A Heavenly Woman
8. Cremation Flats and a Little Grass

CHAPTER 2

GRAND CANYON TEXTS AND SILENCE

Side Canyons
1. What We Bring to the Grand Canyon
2. Reflections on Historic "First View"
3. The Shamanic Sipapu

CHAPTER 3

THE ART OF TURNING AROUND

Side Canyons

1. My First Solo Trip
2. The First Stop
3. The Sublime
4. The Failings of Nature Worship

CHAPTER 4

THE CORRIDOR TRAVAIL

Side Canyons

1. The Grand Canyon's Best Trail
2. Into the Depths
3. The Yucca Cache and a Ranger's Compassion
4. Indian Garden: Creek Cracks and Mulish Water
5. Horn Creek: Taking Note

CHAPTER 5

MONUMENT CANYON TRANSFORMATION

Side Canyons

1. Slot Canyon Intrusion
2. Hermit Without Paper
3. The Ecstasy of Monument Creek: Panology
4. Nature Deficit Disorder

CHAPTER 6

THE CANYON AND CULTURE

Side Canyons

1. Delight and Joy on the Trail
2. Death and Solo Hiking

3. The Sacred Canyon and Profane Users
4. The Native American Vision Quest
5. The Inner and the Outer: Panology

CONCLUSION

BIBLIOGRAPHY

Colorado River

Phantom Ranch

Grand Canyon Village

Hermits Rest

Powell Monument

SCALE IN MILES

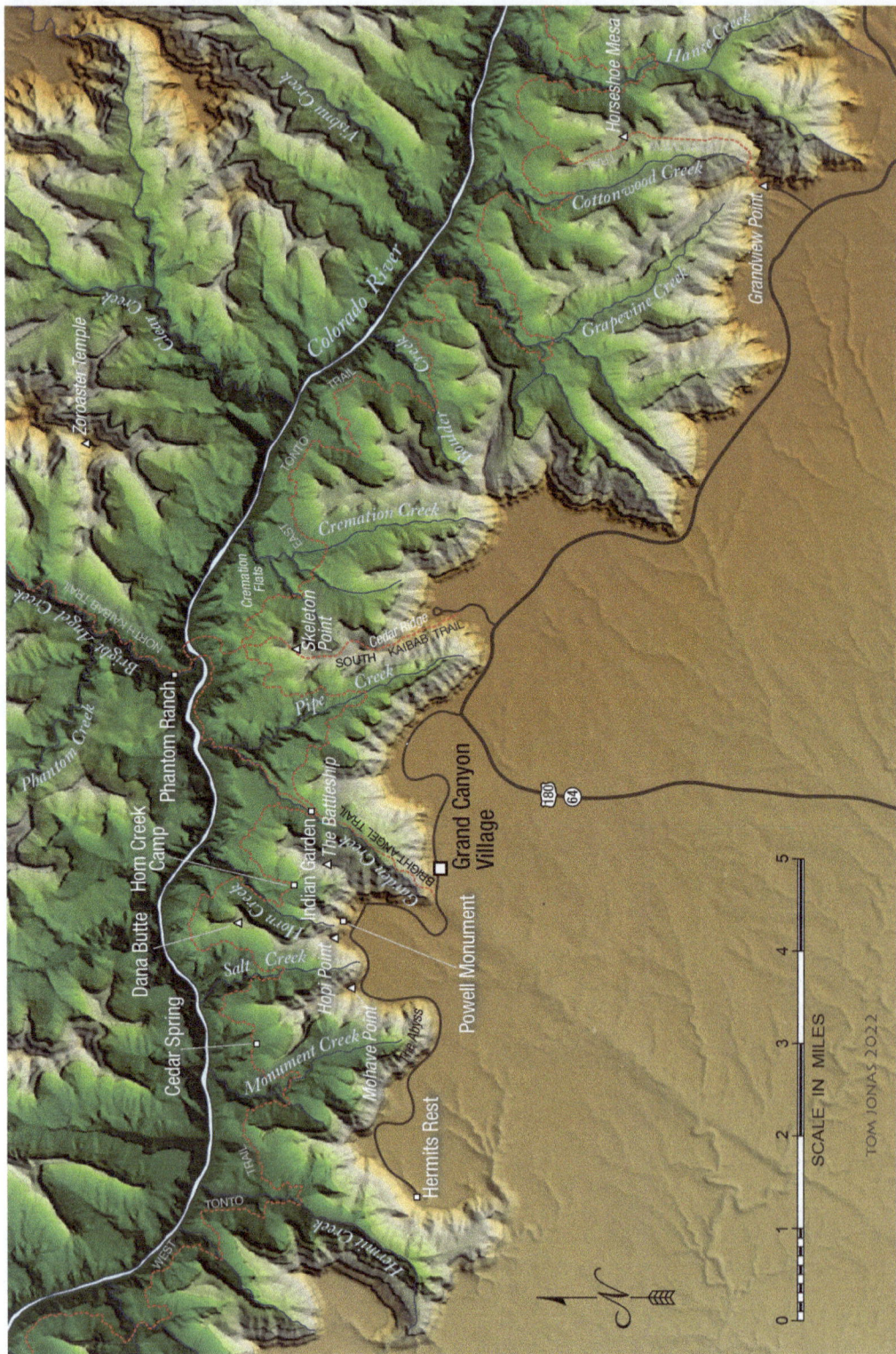

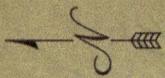

TOM JONAS 2022

PREFACE

On first opening a book, I want to know about the author, specifically what kind of person they are. I want to *feel* the character of the
writer. Then I want to hear things I have never considered before
and to read of experiences I have never had. And so, I give you this
"Preface," to let you know about, or at least get a feel for me, the
author.

As one gets older, time becomes a major priority, but for me, time
seems to have been a priority throughout my life—I am the sort of
guy who attempts many difficult tasks continuously, often simultaneously. To paraphrase Henry David Thoreau, "I want, when upon
my death, to know that I have *really lived*."

In 1992 (already in my fifties) I was struck with the notion that
I was missing my childhood experiences of America's southwest
deserts and mountains. I grew up in the Los Angeles area and our
family vacations consisted of car camping. Later, when I was in high
school, my brother and I designed and built our own backpacks for
back-country backpacking. We visited the deserts often, sometimes
the canyon areas of the Colorado Plateau, and finally experienced
some marvelous, long backpacking in the High Sierras.

It was in the Sierras—specifically at Thousand Island Lake, just
south of the mountain pass from Yosemite National Park—that
I had an unusual experience. I was sitting on a large rock at the
edge of the lake, watching the sunlight dancing on the water that

stretched away to the mountains on the far side. There was a slight breeze that made the water sparkle, like a thousand aspen leaves in the wind. Suddenly, something happened in my head, to my brain, and I felt an extreme delight that mounted to what I would have to call an experience of ecstasy. That word, "ecstasy," means literally to stand outside of oneself. Of all the experiences of my childhood, that one moment stands out to this day. I did not then know that I was destined to have many more such experiences of ecstasy—none of them induced by drugs of any kind.

I am writing this some sixty years after the event, and perhaps you are wondering (as I have often wondered) how it is possible for me to remember the exact feeling and imaginal detail. I found my answer when reading the book of a friend and mentor—*The Soul's Code: In Search of Character and Calling*, by James Hillman (Warner Books, 1996). My childhood soul apparently was laying the groundwork for my experience of nature and how it relates fundamentally to my *psyche*, my soul. Hillman claims that, just as the acorn grows into an oak tree, one's early life experiences grow into what is referred to in the Old Testament as the "Tree of Life." Today, we might say that our early life experiences are of utmost importance in shaping our final stage of life.

Not only does early youth mysteriously determine our destiny, but also along "the inner journey" of life, we experience what feels like magical coincidences (synchronicities) that shape that destiny. It was not until I wrote this book that I realized my experience, my "inner journey," was similar to those of the ancient Native American *shamans*. I now understand that wisdom comes not from books and degrees, but rather from uncontrolled "deep" experiences, which I consider to be common or collective. Considerable space lies between knowledge and wisdom; between spirit and psyche (soul); between science, with its technology, and lived life.

From 1990 to 1996 I went, each March, to hike alone on the Tonto Platform in the Grand Canyon. As I did so, undisturbed by civilized interruptions, my brain was flooded with inner wisdom. I had not planned it—indeed had sought only to absorb the beauty of the Grand Canyon—and it took me a further quarter century to realize that my inner journey was being fundamentally transformed by those six trips. I imagine that this is what Thoreau was referring to when he uttered his famous passage: "In wildness is the preservation of the world."

Inner "wildness" of mind, heart, and soul (to use three traditional metaphors) coupled with our hands, feet, eyes, and ears focused on the outward wildness of wilderness, leads to transformation.

I now recognize that my hiking trips of the 1990s addressed my "midlife crisis" and evoked my rite of passage from middle to old age, leading me to feel that old age is the *best* of all phases of life, despite the weakening of body and the coming of eventual death. Old age is the soulful aspect of life and wisdom.

I had, by my fifties, been teaching philosophy for three decades and would continue to do so for another ten years while also creating a land-development company that aimed to put environmental sensitivity at the heart of all we did. In 2008, I retired from teaching and, within a few years, also closed the company. Eventually, some years later, I started writing this book, using my "trail notes" and simple recollection. I discovered a "coherence" of place and thought that astonished me, and I found a term for it: "topographic spirituality," where "spirituality" is used loosely, not religiously.

Years before Plato, Heraclitus claimed that the psyche is unlimited and can never be reached and explored entirely by the rational mind: "If you travel every path, you will not find the limits of the Psyche; so deep is its Logos." (Heraclitus, Fragment 45). Such is a blow to the ego, the rational mind of self-preservation! However, such overcoming of *hubris* rewards one with an affiliation to psyche, a "deep" place, corresponding to the Grand Canyon's depths. The psychic transformation from adult rationality to psychological association within the depth of human experience brings joy and even ecstasy, which can never be matched in the middle stage of life, no matter how happy we are.

As a professor of philosophy in Boston for more than forty years, I learned that, on the whole, my students knew little or nothing of the natural world. I took them on field trips to Walden Pond—Thoreau's retreat into reality—and for walks through Boston's Common and Public Garden and asked them to identify the trees and flowers we encountered. Generally, they would know only one or two species of trees—usually the maples—and a few more flowers. I asked them why trees are important for human life, and none of them knew that trees take in carbon dioxide and give off oxygen. I asked if trees have any philosophical meaning. Invariably I was met with bewilderment: "Philosophical? Trees?" I would respond that trees, especially those such as the towering examples on the Common, are seen by Native Americans to be "centering," as in "The Tree of Life" or the "Tree of the Fruit of Good and Evil," or "The Tree of Gnosis." Time and again, my students would ask: "What is gnosis?" And so, I decided to create a course—both undergraduate and graduate—called, simply, "Gnosticism."

As a younger man I had studied at the University of Chicago with Mircea Eliade (1907–1986), then the world's expert on shamanism. It was Eliade who set my Ph.D. exam, not directly on shamanism, but rather, on "primitive mentality." I wondered if it were possible for non-Native people to have firsthand knowledge of a shaman's experience, and I found this:

> The last Havasupai shaman died in the early 1960s. Some mourning ceremonies, borrowed from the Mojave, were sung at funerals, but these, too, were attenuated offerings. A harvest festival, known as the Peach Festival, continues, but this is now primarily a social affair. — Carma Lee Smithson & Robert C. Euler, *Havasupai Legends: Religion and Mythology of the Havasupai Indians of the Grand Canyon* (University of Utah Press, 1994)

To this I would add Mircea Eliade:

Willard Park [*Shamanism in Western North America*] defines North American shamanism by the supernatural power that the shaman acquires as the result of a direct personal experience. "This power is generally manipulated in such a way as to be a matter of concern to others in the society. Accordingly, the practice of witchcraft may be as important a part of shamanism as the curing of disease or the charming of game in a communal hunt." We will designate by the term of shamanism, then, all the practices by which supernatural power may be acquired by mortals, the exercise of that power either for good or evil, and all the concepts and beliefs associated with these practices.

—Mircea Eliade, *Shamanism: Archaic Techniques of Ecstasy*
(Bollingen Series LXXVI, Pantheon Books, 1964)

It is expected that scholars will place the "supernatural power" that one can experience, in the context of their society; but from my own ecstatic experiences, it is clear to me that our contemporary secular society is tremendously different from that of the ancient shamans.

So how are we to demonstrate "supernatural power" in our society, a society in which the only such demonstrable power comes from an atomic weapon?

I believe that solitude, while not a guarantee, is nevertheless essential if one is to experience ecstasy... solitude and "deep-nature absorption."

Here is an example of what deep-nature-absorption experience can do for you, revealed by a man of the nineteenth century who died at the age of forty-five. He and his brother were boating up a river in New Hampshire. After beaching the boat, and settling in for a night's sleep, they both heard a drummer across the woods practicing militia music. One of the brothers then wrote:

When we are in health, all sounds fife and drum for us: we hear the notes of music in the air, or catch its echoes dying away when we awake in the dawn. Marching is when the pulse of the hero beats in unison with the pulse of Nature, and he steps to the measure of the universe; then there is true courage and invincible strength. [...] These simple sounds related us to the stars. Aye, there was a logic in them so convincing that the combined sense of mankind could never make me doubt their conclusions. *I stop my habitual thinking, as if the plow had suddenly run deeper in its furrow through the crust of the world.* How can I go on, who have just stepped over such a bottomless skylight in the bog of my life. [my italics]

This passage, from Henry David Thoreau's *A Week on the Concord and Merrimack Rivers* (Princeton University Press, 1983) has become known as the "Different Drummer's Passage" and is often misunderstood. It is *not* a declaration of New England individuality or "Transcendentalism." Thoreau (1817–1862) is not advocating his own individual beat: rather he wishes to keep to the beat of Nature. In the same book, Thoreau also refers to what I call "panology":

In my Pantheon, Pan still reigns in his pristine glory, with his ruddy face, his flowing beard, and his shaggy body, his pipe and his crook, his nymph Echo, and his chosen daughter Iambe; for the great God Pan is not dead, as was rumored. No god ever dies. Perhaps of all the gods of New England and of ancient Greece, I am most constant at his shrine.

The nineteenth-century Thoreau met with Pan on the Merrimack River. In the twentieth century, I found him beside Monument Creek in the Grand Canyon. What follows is an exploration of what that encounter meant to me and how it framed my philosophy of the inner journey.

GRAND CANYON ECSTASY

Hikers descend the South Kaibab Trail on a fall morning with the shadows of broken clouds sailing over the Grand Canyon. *Photo by Gary Ladd.*

CHAPTER 1

CREMATION IN Z-FLAT

Side Canyons
. . . .

1. Descent into Muddy Waters

2. The Miracle Cave Rock

3. The First Shelter

4. Raven Wash

5. Grapevine's Stone Time

6. Scout Leader Dynamics

7. A Heavenly Woman

8. Cremation Flats and a Little Grass

March, 1994. I leave Boston, Massachusetts, fly to Phoenix, Arizona, and then drive a rental car to the Grand Canyon. I arrive at the Bright Angel Lodge to learn that there has been a break in the water pipe from Roaring Springs, and both the Bright Angel Trail and South Kaibab Trail are closed to hikers. Despite my backpacking reservation, I am shut out of my trip and am devastated. Unbeknownst to me, the Backpacker's Reservation Office (now the Backcountry Information Center) had called my house in Massachusetts to let me know of the closures. They had forgotten, or perhaps did not know, that the journey from Massachusetts to the South Rim of the Grand Canyon takes a whole day and so had called after I left. I am at a loss. Cremation and Grapevine have water, so why close the trails for *everyone* because the Bright Angel Campground and Phantom Ranch don't have water? I have no desire to go to either of those locations, so why am I shut out? The ranger at the Backpacker's Office tells me that his colleague will stop me going beyond Cedar Ridge. I plead with him. I am going to Cremation. He is unmovable: "It doesn't matter; the trail is closed to everyone."

I go to the bar for a beer and to consider my options. There is no way I am going to be grounded. I decide to prepare, packing my backpack after dinner with the assumption that either the water pipe will be repaired and no ranger will stop me at Cedar Ridge, or I will simply lie and go around them. They are not going to stop me from going to Cremation. No way. I will go no matter what.

1. Descent into Muddy Waters

It was just after 10:00 a.m. when I parked my car at Kaibab Point (no longer allowed) and, after a short walk to the trailhead to the south, began the descent of the South Kaibab Trail. It was in shadow as far as the ridge, and the sky was overcast. It looked like rain, but not immediately, so I should be down to Cremation before it started.

I had my pack rain cover on and was wearing rain gear—my heavy rain jacket with rain paints, since it was also quite cold. It felt good to get on the trail. And, with all the closures, there was almost no one on the trail. Nor did there seem to be any trail ice, although the mules apparently got there ahead of me, so there were plenty of bright green, fresh globs of mule "residuals," here and there. I cursed them—besides their deposits, they were making holes in the trail. The South Kaibab Trail was a "maintained" trail, so why the mules? (Apparently, today, the mules are on the South Kaibab Trail only in the afternoons and are used not for carrying humans but for transporting garbage from Phantom Ranch—the heart of the Grand Canyon National Park.)

The South Kaibab Trail has some of the best views in the park. After the short switchbacks just below the trailhead, the trail follows Cedar Ridge straight out into the heart of the Grand Canyon. Very soon after descending from the Rim it straightens out and descends moderately, until an outcropping of rock slabs, which I call Windy Point—in 1991 I had to lie down on the rocks to avoid being blown off the trail with my too-big backpack. Now, three years later, my pack was more modest, and packed more tightly, with the rain cover helping to keep everything together and allow the wind to blow over it more easily. Wind or no wind, the view was spectacular, and I paused to take it in.

I looked at the sky and hoped for the sun to break out, but it still looked like rain. I set off again and took the switchback that immediately doubles back to the south; the descent increased dramatically but was still quite manageable. That switchback opens a good view of the Pipe Springs drainage, and a little further I took a large switchback on the east side of the ridge and had an excellent view into the top part of the west side of the Cremation Drainage, where I was headed. The trail was red dirt all the way, with laid stones in some places, and short pines providing some shade.

Now the trail straightened out again and passed into the Cedar Ridge outhouses and mule rest area. There was no water here, but it was a good place to stop and rest—downhill with a big backpack is always hardest on the legs when they must work to hold both load and body back against gravity. Uphill relies on aerobic training—which every backpacker does extensively—and walking at a steady pace to avoid getting winded.

Before this trip, I had done lots of work on the stair climber—turning backwards to train for the downhills, but I wanted to be in good shape for the next day so knew I had to go slowly and take a significant rest, with my feet propped up higher than my head, in order to deal with the lactic acid buildup that was inevitable.

Two years earlier, I had hiked to Bright Angel Creek in one day, but this year, I would find a place to camp in Cremation. I took a full half hour at the Ridge stop, first taking in the view, then using the toilet, then eating and drinking, and finally finding a log upon which to raise my feet.

At this point, amazingly, I had yet to see another person. There was no ranger preventing me from going out to Skeleton Point, to begin the cobblestone switchbacks of the steep descent through the Redwall. As I had suspected, the office was concerned with back-packers headed to Phantom Ranch, while those connecting to the Tonto Trail, like me, were irrelevant.

From the Cedar Ridge rest area, the trail makes its descent entirely on the east side of the ridge, skirting O'Neill Butte, which looms straight ahead. One short switchback is enough to get around the flank of O'Neill, and then there is an amazingly straight trail that takes one out on the middle of the ridge as it stretches to Skeleton Point, at about 5,200ft elevation. But, as always in the Grand

Canyon, what you gain by a straight trail, you will pay for immediately afterward.

As I loaded up again at Skeleton Point, I scanned the sky. It was filling with dark clouds. I tightened my pack rain cover and swung it on my pack. "Well," I thought, "perhaps the rain will wash the stone dust off the cobblestones and give me some surer footing." I was well prepared for wet weather, so thought I should be all right.

Then it began to rain.

It was the first rain I had ever experienced in the Grand Canyon in March, and it was soon pouring. Nevertheless, I made it down the switchbacks, and soon after, returned to the almost straight and wide trail descending toward the Tonto plateau. It had turned to mud, already inches thick and very slippery, a far greater hazard than the dusty cobblestones. The mule hooves, with their metal shoes, had ground the small gravel clods into a thick layer of fine dirt, and the rain had done the rest.

I had brought two walking sticks this trip, and several times fell down, pack and all, so that my left arm had to aid the Leki in my right hand to catch myself before I fell off the trail. In my right hand I was also carrying my umbrella. No guidebook had warned of the danger of this deep mud at the very *beginning* of a rainstorm. I carefully moved back and forth from side to side of the trail to avoid the deepest of the mud. Time and again, sometimes just 50ft below the previous time, I stopped and tried to figure out the safest way down through all the mud and water. The rain was not the problem. Indeed, everywhere in the canyon, the porous rock absorbs water well on the trails. But the years of mule traffic had created a quagmire.

Towards the bottom of this muddy slope—now christened "Muddy Waters"—the trail began to look like one of those California mud slides. I thought of leaving the trail and making my own way down toward Cremation to the east, rather than following the trail that goes mostly to the north. But I decided against it because the likelihood of disturbing a snake or falling on the rather steep slope and tumbling down until I hit a rock with my body, was too high a risk. The slope on the trail was not nearly as steep as over its side, so I opted for caution and decided to follow the trail to the bottom. Even so, I attempted to follow a middle course, picking my way between off-trail and the middle of the trail where the mud was the deepest. As much as possible I tried to walk beside the trail to avoid the mud on my left and the bushes on my right. It was slow going, and all the way down I thought about those damned mules—they'll get you on the slippery cobblestones and in the muddy waters. Either way, they'll get you!

2. The Miracle Cave Rock

At the junction of South Kaibab and Tonto East, I turned east. This was as far as I had been toward Cremation before, so from here on, the trail was unfamiliar to me. But I was finally off the mule trail and the ground was firm, despite its flatness and the hard rain pouring down.

The trail took me down into and out of two consecutive washes, and after a bit of flat, made a straight-line descent, due east, over a pile of rocks that seemed to go on and on. The rain must have added 10lb or 15lb to my load, and since I was packed for more than a week, it had weighed about 60lb when I started. I was soaked, exhausted, and dreading what lay ahead: putting up my tent in the pouring rain or crouching beneath my tent tarp until the rain stopped, all in the wide-open spaces of the Cremation trail.

I made my way slowly down the rock-strewn slope, where there was no place to set up camp and I was still exposed to the weather. But I knew that I had to stop walking in this downpour with this heavy load! As I approached the end of the rocky slope, I saw, to my left, a very flat area, the flattest I had ever seen on the Tonto, and I could just make out the outline of a circle of flat stones, indicating an impromptu campground. But it looked muddy, and I had already had enough mud for a lifetime. I looked, instead, to the right where the trails took a sharp turn to the south, and saw that it continued down, which should mean less exposure to the wind. I trudged on. I was having a hard time seeing through my glasses, with the water and pieces of mud stuck to them. I knew that, very soon, I would have to give up and stop, wherever I was. I was exhausted and getting colder by the moment, despite the energy I was burning as I walked. I wondered if I was close to hypothermia. I noticed, when I stopped, that I was shivering—a bad sign. If I stopped walking now, how could I warm myself while cuddled under my tarp? I needed shelter so I could start my camp stove.

I crossed another little drainage and could now clearly see, through the rain, the rims of Cremation, a couple thousand feet away. I climbed a small slope and again knew that I must stop very soon, as this was too much for this no-longer-young man! Who ever heard of such rain at this time of year, the middle of March? I was beyond tired, cold, and apparently condemned to sleep in a wet tent and sleeping bag, with no way to dry out on that bleak slope of Cremation. I was becoming afraid, but despite my fear, I noticed the irony: the trail was closed because of a water pipe, and here I had way too much water! There was no doubt about it, I was at a low point in my Grand Canyon journey. But I must not wallow in self-pity; I had to deal with my hypothermia.

The rain, though no longer a downpour, continued to fall steadily. I needed a shelter of some kind desperately. Maybe a small tree where I could rig up my ground tarp to make an emergency tent coverage with my rope. If I couldn't get dry, then at night when the air became even colder, I could go into a true hypothermic state. I knew that I could get ischemic brain damage if I was hypothermic for too long, and I was approaching that now—I had to stop soon and get warm, somehow. I could cover both myself and my backpack with my tarp, but as the sun went down, it would be cold even if the rain stopped. And even if the rain did eventually stop, how was I going to dry off my body, when everything in my pack must be soaked? Fear of dying began to enter my mind and I told myself not to panic.

As I went down the other side of the slope, I saw below me what appeared to be a complete anomaly—a gigantic boulder with no other stones around it. It was lying by itself at the edge of the trail, and as I came closer, I stared at it while catching my breath. It was as big as a small house and appeared to have a small indentation on its east side. The rain was coming from the west. I picked up my pace, despite my body yelling at me to stop.

When I was about 40 ft from the boulder, I saw that there was, indeed, a hole on the east side. Perhaps it would provide me shelter of sorts. I pushed on and realized that it was not just a hole, it was a *big* hole. I increased my stride until I was almost running. A cave! The hole was a cave! It was only about 5ft deep, but at least 10ft wide. I had to duck to get my back-packed frame under the lip of the entrance, but there I collapsed on my back, face up, backpack below me, on *dry, soft soil*! I had found the Waldorf Astoria in the Grand Canyon! I yelled out: "I can't believe it!"

At last, I removed my pack, leaned it against the cave's back side, and then noticed an arrangement of rocks with which to make a small fireplace. Then, I realized that the water dripping off my pack was turning the floor of the cave into mud. Quickly, I pulled out my tent tarp, opened it up, and spread the dry side over the sandy soil. I placed my pack and raincoat at one end of the tarp, then got out my WhisperLite stove and gas tank and worked feverishly to get it pumped. I almost prayed for the wooden match to light, earnestly hoping that the "waterproof" container had kept the matches dry. If I couldn't light the stove, I still might die.

My hands were shaking as I struck the first match. It broke in two and fell to the tarp without firing. I grabbed the next match, and struck it slowly, knowing that my life depended upon getting the stove going. It burst into flame, I put it against the stove's gas holes, and turned the knob—I had fire! I quickly poured some of my drinking water into the pot, put that on the fire, got out my drinking cup, and hoped that the heat of some hot chocolate would bring my core temperature back up, and that the calories in the chocolate would give me some energy. I knew that I must get out of my soaking clothes but decided I would first have two cups of hot chocolate before looking for what might be little better than damp clothes. I thought, "Heat in my stomach first, then deal with my wet skin, if I can."

I stared at the fire, rubbing my hands, and then putting them as close to the stove as possible without injury, rubbing some more, then more heat. And all the while I was thinking: "What a miracle that this shelter is here, and I found it close to the end of my store of energy. This was a close call. But I must keep my gas stove going until my body temp gets up."

This Hole-in-the-Rock spot had obviously served many before, for there were stones all over the outside area, and there was an obvious, leveled off, clear, sandy tent space in front of the cave. My water was now close to a boil; I added the chocolate powder to my cup, poured some water into it, swiveled the cup, since I hadn't taken out the spoon yet, and took a sip—not warm enough! I put the coffee pot back on the fire—noticing that my hands were still shaking from the cold—then took out my sleeping bag, which was a little damp, laid it across the stones at the back of the cave, fished for my camp towel and a change of clothes, along with an extra fleece top and pants, put them on another rock at the back, and went back to the now-hot chocolate. I drank it as quickly as I could to get the maximum benefit from its heat. I put on more water to boil, stripped off all my clothes, wiped myself thoroughly with the camp towel, and quickly dressed in my not-quite-dry replacement clothes. Incredibly, in about two minutes, I was dry for the first time since leaving Skeleton Point. I was still shivering, but the panic was subsiding. After drinking the second hot chocolate, I was "alive" again.

As I warmed up slowly, I realized that my predicament was, in part, of my own making, for I had taken too much time at Cedar Ridge and Skeleton Point. Now, I wondered, "What if there had been no miracle Cave Rock? Would I have made it without a shelter? Who knows? Probably, not."

I thought about the boulder: "What had caused it to roll down the slope, and how was the cave created in its side?" Perhaps the cave had been carved out by water over the course of millions of years. Perhaps an earthquake had dislodged it and sent it rolling down to this place. I had no answer, but in my mind, I hummed Bob Dylan's "Like a Rolling Stone."

From my vantage point within the cave, I looked out at Cremation. It seemed so barren; there appeared to be no large vegetation, nothing that could serve either as shade from the sun or shelter from the rain. It must be very hot in summer, Maybe that was why they named it "Cremation." I was now understanding what it meant to have crossed into a "primitive" area, out of the corridor/threshold that had been my stomping ground until now. And yet, I was only a few miles, perhaps only four, from the South Kaibab Trail.

I finished the hot chocolate and put more water into the pot to boil. Finally, after my third hot drink, I felt human again. But there was now much to do. It was about 5:00 p.m. and I had to see if the tent was dry or at least only mildly damp. I checked it out while making my dinner; it was far from bone dry but not too bad. Lightning was flashing down the canyon to the east, miles away but big, again and again. I ate dinner and hoped for a sunny day tomorrow, for I wouldn't be able to dry the tent entirely without the sun. Now, with food in my stomach, a dry body, and a drying tent, I realized that the rain was easing up and, at last, some blue sky was emerging to the far east. My fear and sorrow were replaced by joy and gratitude: I had survived to explore the Tonto East trail.

Imagine, I would live to fight another day! I had nature to thank for putting this gigantic boulder here, but the fact that I had found it was pure luck.

3. The First Shelter

As I awoke to a calm, sunny morning, I was dreaming of caves. I opened my eyes and stared at the cave's wall, recalling the wall of the Minaret miner's shack in the High Sierras. Both surfaces were vividly in my mind, one now before my eyes, the other in my memory from almost thirty years earlier. This is what a deep-nature-absorption experience does to memory: it plants indelible images that stay with us until the end of life.

Now another image came to mind, of the board surface of a playhouse shack I built when I was about ten or twelve years old, in our backyard in Inglewood, California. It was the first of many shelters I built. And as I write this, the playhouse reoccurs, as if it lived in a timeless realm of my imagination, having to do with some primary, "primordial architecture" of the psyche. I ask, are shelters for protecting the body, or can they be about sheltering the psyche, inducing a certain "love of house"? That love of house is what I call "panological architecture," the building of shelter with the psyche dictating its features.

I have built parts, or the whole, of five houses in my life, and many more in my imagination, as part of an exploratory proposed investment, in the attempt to unravel the mystery of which characteristics establish that feeling of "enclosure," of shelter, of "home"—a place of loving joy, where one would choose to die in peace when the time comes.

Mankind's first shelter was undoubtedly in caves, which they did not make but may have cleared from debris and then painted the walls. Humans must "mark" their territory, just as other animals do. Now I, too, had discovered the peace of a cave shelter.

The sun was out, just over the eastern horizon up the canyon, and was shining through the opening in the boulder, onto its inner surface of curves and indentations and cracks. I admired them as I breathed and drank my morning coffee. The primitiveness of Cave Rock, and the barrenness of this sweep of the Tonto Trail, somehow evoked what Jung and Eliade called "archetypal."

I returned to my sleeping bag. I was still exhausted from my perilous descent and needed more rest.

The morning sun swept up the trail after cresting Horseshoe

Mesa and reached my tent with its comforting light just as I turned over and went back to sleep for another hour. When I awoke, I made coffee again and drank it with some crackers and peanut butter while I reviewed my notes from the previous night, scratched on my little pads, with the help of my sidekick, Fleischmann's Whiskey. Then, I tucked back into my sleeping bag to daydream.

In my scribblings the night before I had referenced Nietzsche's "death of God" in relation to how Christianity had mixed into its myths a good deal of ego. Inevitably, Christians think of Nietzsche, if they have heard of him, as the enemy, and his notion of the "death of God" is taken literally—even though Gods, by definition, don't die. Nietzsche tells the story of "The Madman" in *The Joyful Wisdom*. The madman jumps into a crowd in the marketplace and asks where has God gone? Most of the people in the marketplace, Nietzsche tells us, do not believe in God. They answer the madman by suggesting that God is lost, or has strayed away like a child, or keeps himself hidden, or is afraid of unbelievers, or has taken a sea-voyage, or emigrated.

Our culture only hears the proclamation that "God is dead." We think the madman (i.e., Nietzsche) is an atheist criticizing believers. But if you read the above carefully, Nietzsche doesn't criticize, he condemns! It isn't that the belief in God is nonsense—far from it, Nietzsche equates God with the Sun, the center of all life and the source of human stability. I read this passage to mean that so-called religious people "killed God" because they wanted outer miracle (literal history), mystery (dogma to replace questions), and authority (the Vatican's pretensions). Thus, believers changed the Judaeo-Christian religion by exalting themselves into God's place, and such god-like egos turned Christianity into its major heresy—first practiced by St. Paul—of "sado-masochistic gnosticism." From that, all nations learned to start wars or protect themselves from others who do so.

Nietzsche was born in 1844, when a group of evangelical Christians expected the apocalypse; what they got, instead, was Friedrich Nietzsche. He died in 1900. The century that followed him was (and continues to be in the next century) a period in which god-like egos rampage over all others in search of gnostic power, power based on the killing of God, the Father Archetype, and replacing him with their self-righteousness, covering their desire to transform human nature after their own images.

The sun was warming my tent and even the sleeping bag within it. But my mind was preoccupied with first Nietzsche and then caves. I thought of Plato's Cave, in *The Republic*; Fletcher's *The Man from the Cave* (1981); "Plato's Cave" in the basement of a Boston juice bar, where I would read students' papers and discuss philosophy with them; the cave at the bottom of Thoreau's Falls in New Hampshire; and finally, the prehistoric caves I had contemplated on many a night, thanks to the photographs of the likes of archaeologist David Lewis-Williams (1934–). All of this raced through my mind that morning, evoked by one line written into my trail notes the night before: "CAVE>FORM." It meant that a cave, like all objects and notions (justice, love, truth, beauty, etc.) has what Plato called a "Form," and what Jung called "an archetypal image."

Scientific epistemology theorizes that we experience objects and that each time we do, we compare the object with another until we identify that group of similar objects by one word: sun, stone, tree, lake, river, etc. Plato, on the other hand, thinks that the higher epis-temology—that above his famous "Divided Line"—is the opposite: first we know of the Form or Archetypal Image, and then we apply such to every object within the group of same objects. Plato argues that we know a cave only after our psyches experience the Form or Idea and then apply it to various objects. The Form is known by *noesis* and not by trust or imagination, nor, I add, by consen-sus. How does one know of Fatherhood? Not by interviewing or experiencing various fathers and then generalizing. For Plato, one must learn about Fatherhood and then, knowing its essence, one can determine which men are real fathers and which are not.

How does one know Truth? Truth is not determined by consen-sus or surveys, nor by any such data, but rather by climbing outside of Plato's famous and misunderstood cave. Those in the cave see shadows of objects rather than the real thing; they must climb out of the cave and into the sunlight to perceive real forms or ideas. In other words, Plato's cave is a metaphor of popular misunderstanding, whereas to climb outside of it, is to become wise.

The love of wisdom, called philosophy, is no such thing until one can determine that Plato's cave is a sort of test on one's psyche. Jung, in my opinion, used Plato when he determined to apply the metaphor of shadow to that of the psyche's evil or mistaken side, since each component of the collective unconscious, all the archetypes, have the potential for good or evil. Shadow thinking is evil, whereas thinking in the sunlight of what Plato called "the leaping flame" (the Seventh Letter) creates philosophy, the love of wisdom.

Jung believed that when the conscious mind assimilates the deeper unconscious, one of two things will happen: ecstasy, if the mind has prepared itself for such a thing, and pathology, if the mind is unprepared. Jung learned from Plato's Forms and applied them to all things "archetypal," such as falling in love. The "falling" suggests that its source is the collective unconscious—the falling moves the psyche into the "lower" place of the collective unconscious, and in response, the collective unconscious presents what Jung called "the anima"—as in that part of a woman that "fits well" with a man's feminine aspect.

Plato perceived the ancient Greek sophists as living in a "cave" of epistemological blindness—a cultural cave that separated them from the life of sun-lit nature on the earth's crust, what Thoreau called "heaven." (Apparently then, today's millennials have put themselves in cultural caves—not subterranean ones, rather "flying caves" called "airplanes," and forms of superficial social contacts, called "smart" phones. They play virtual reality games because they have never had or recollected a deep-nature absorption.)

Nomadism is often typical of modern Americans; they lack the centering that underlies the Native American notion of the *sipapu*, the center place from which one has come, and to which one returns, in reverence. The Navaho notion of the place of emergence can be demythologized into the emergence of the collective unconscious in their tribal cultures. The nomadic American must often move from one place to another, from one relationship to another, from a cold climate to a hot one and vice versa according to the time of year. The opposite of this nomadic state of mind is panology, the philosophy of "placidness," of being "somewhere" rather than "out in nowhere."

After finally emerging from my sleeping bag and shelter, I decided that I would not abandon this site—which in a sense had saved my life—until the next morning. I had written two nights into my itinerary for Cremation, and with a camping-at-large designation, I could spend them both here, at Cave Rock, before walking on to the Grapevine district. By staying put I would be in better shape and more fully recovered from the previous day's ordeal. I decided to lay everything out in the sun to dry and to check out the first of the three main tributaries of Cremation, to see if there were any good pools from which to collect water.

Thus, I laid everything out to dry in the morning's sun, stowed my canteens in my backpack and, armed with my walking sticks, went beyond Cave Rock to the edge of the first of three canyons that merge to make Cremation Canyon. I had to climb down cautiously, using cairns (stones piled up to indicate the trail), all the way to the bottom. Despite the rains of the day before, there was very little water in the creek bed—not enough to filter—so I went on to the second canyon, which also was almost dry. I continued to the third drainage, which was less of a canyon and more of an open river, which I would have to cross the next day. I was glad I had decided to spend another day west of this drainage, for maybe after another twenty-four hours the water would be lower and more easily traversed. Fortunately, the drainage was wide and so the current was slow. I didn't want to suffer another wetting, and surely there wouldn't be a second Cave Rock in the canyon.

I turned back after filling my canteens. I would take my time and go carefully down and back up the two canyons, but I was anxious to get back to Cave Rock because I had left my tent up to claim the site—never before had I left my tent so far away. What if someone stole it? It wasn't likely, but what if someone decided to take over the site and move the tent up or down the trail? Then I realized how foolish I was being—there was no one but me in this part of the Canyon. I castigated myself for being so skeptical of others, and besides, any backpacker who left the Kaibab trailhead this morning would not be down to Cremation until much later in the day. Nevertheless, after carrying my tent all over the Plateau, I irrationally felt uneasy to be separated from it.

Despite my fears, I forced myself to take my time. I had all day to recuperate, and I wanted to be ready for the next day's long walk to Lonetree or beyond. I crossed the bed of the middle canyon but couldn't find the start of the trail on the other side. Most often there are cairns on both sides of a canyon, but I could find none on the west side and saw no sign of a trail marking. All was boulders and large rocks, there was no visible dirt, and so I had left no footprints. I knew then that I should have made a cairn when I reached the bottom going the other way, but I had not thought of it. I returned to the east side and tried to find my earlier footprints there, but all I saw where the ones I had just made. I felt a frisson of fear at the thought of climbing out of the canyon without the trail and then having to find the trail at the top. I had learned a lesson—look for cairns and where there are none, set up your own.

I sat down on a rock on the creek's west side, relaxed myself, and tried not to panic. I tried to remember if earlier I had crossed pretty much straight, or at an angle. I decided it was at an angle. I walked that angle to the canyon side, stood on the highest stone I could find, and noticed a bit of dirt about 10ft above me and to my left. I scrambled toward it, and at last found the elusive trail. I built a small but recognizable cairn and went back up to join the trail at the top. When at last I spotted Cave Rock, it was like coming home.

Of course, when I did get back, not only was the boulder there, but so, too, was the tent, just where I had left "her," but drier. I took a drink of water, sat down on one of the small flat rocks beneath the cave overhang, and surveyed my surroundings. Having been alone since starting down the South Kaibab Trail, I felt that things were shifting in my mind. If only my solitude would continue a few more days. Thanks to the Roaring Springs pipe break, it was quite probable that I would see no one for quite a while.

One of the first things that happens when you are alone for more than a day or so is that you start talking to yourself, or think more about yourself because no one is around to look at you or draw their own conclusions about you. I have always talked to my daemon, that which connects me to my unconscious. And, when lonely, I talk to my wife, as if the air will send the message across the country to her ear.

Imagination is so much freer in the canyon because there are no interruptions, unless, of course, you interrupt yourself. At Cave Rock I was already getting used to this change of mind. I clambered into the cave and made myself a bowl of cereal, using the little boxes of orange juice as my liquid—my daughter, who was trying to convert me to veganism, had recommended orange juice for cereal when soy milk was not available—it was not cold, but it served its purpose. Still feeling the need to recover from my hypothermic scramble of the day before, I decided to walk, without my pack, around the immediate area, and then to get an early start in the morning in order to make it to Grapevine, if I could. Two nights at Cave Rock was a luxury I felt I deserved.

The next day dawned bright and sunny. I sat in the sand beside my tent, facing north. Zoroaster Temple towered over Cremation across the Colorado River. I stared at it, an almost perfect three-dimensional triangle. I knew there was Clear Creek Trail on the other side of the Inner Gorge, which started at the North Bright Angel Trail just above Phantom Ranch, and then circled around Zoroaster Temple to Clear Creek on its east side, crossed Zoroaster Canyon and headed to the base of the Ottoman Amphitheater. But then I looked east, down the slight slope in front of Cave Rock toward the rim of Cremation Creek. I noticed a small drainage, filled with sand, winding down to the drop-off into Cremation Canyon. I made up my mind: I would explore that. There would surely be a good view of the Cremation Canyon from that dry creek's drop-off and just as surely, I would not run into any other visitors!

4. Raven Wash

Within fifteen minutes of starting out, I came to the end of the sand-laden drainage and crossed the last 10ft of the wash, which was all rock. I was right: from there I had an excellent view of the Cremation Canyon where its three drainages merge together. I could now clearly see the wide third drainage with its foot-deep water spread out perhaps 50ft below me. From where I now stood, it was just a small ribbon and I could only see a small bit of it, since here the canyon was wide but curved with small hills below the steep cliffs. To my left was the curvature of the walls that made up its west rim, an impressive string of stone. I got down on my knees and crawled to about 5ft from the drop-off, where I could comfortably sit and take in the view. The canyon was so large, it was obvious that a tremendous amount of water must come roaring through every now and then. Trekkers like to go down these canyons as far as possible, even when there may be rain on the plateau above. Fall is the most dangerous time to hike the side canyons of the Colorado, but early spring, when there is still snow on the South Rim, is also dangerous, even when a weather forecast calls for no rain. From my vantage point at the narrow end of the Cremation wash I could see the vastness of the side canyon. I was, at once, seeing intimacy and immensity—Bachelard's binary relationship—laid out before me.

I got out my trail snacks, mostly peanuts, and washed them down with my canteen's water when a black raven swooped down and landed on a small rock bench about 10ft from, and maybe 3ft above me. Canyon rules state that you should not feed the wildlife, but I was on my second day of isolation from any human and concluded that I needed a companion for a while. In Native American religion, the raven is known as the Trickster, and I identified with the bird.

I was not sure that the raven would eat my peanuts, but I tossed one towards it, but about a foot below its current perch. Immediately, the bird hopped down, but then looked at me as if seeking permission to eat. Then the bird turned fully sideways to me as if to keep one eye on me even as it looked at the peanut with its other eye. It picked it up and ate. I tossed a second peanut but made sure it landed about 2ft closer to me. The bird took a few steps toward me, looked at the peanut, then at me, and then took another few steps before once again turning sideways to pick up the peanut while keeping one eye focused on me. I threw a third peanut about 4ft away, and the same thing happened: steps, looking up at me, more steps, sideways turn, then picking up the peanut before flying back to its original perch on the upper bench.

The bird reminded me that there are people from whom I, too, wished to stay 10ft away—we might share an academic interest, but we were not necessarily friends. Nevertheless, I wondered how close the bird would come if tempted. Could I bring it all the way?

I stretched out my hand, with a peanut in it, and looked at the raven, which hopped down the benches again, and came to within about 4ft of me. I dropped the peanut straight down, pulled my arm in, and waited for the bird to go for it. He did, now only about 2½ft from me, but again with the sideways approach.

Then, to my surprise, another raven swooped down and landed a short distance from us. I stared at the two birds. The first was a little bigger than the second, so I called it Romeo and the newcomer Juliet. I threw a peanut toward the newcomer, and she gobbled it down.

Then I threw her a second—after all, she had some catching up to do. This time, both birds went for it. They arrived at the same time and Romeo took a peck at Juliet, winning the peanut by force. It was a typical show of superior strength, but subtle female advances had me favoring Juliet. I threw a peanut to her other side, away from Romeo, and she quickly grabbed it. Romeo looked at me as if he had lost a good friend. How dare Juliet move in on his territory?

I ate some M&Ms from my trail snack and pondered the new situation. I decided to feed Romeo again, since he was the one who had braved proximity for benevolence, at least up to almost 2ft. So, I dropped a peanut just in front of me, within arm's length, and stared at the bird as if to say, "the peanut is in your court." Romeo made the same approaching procedure, but stopped at about 2ft, turned sideways, and waited. I looked at Juliet who had also approached, but to my left and about 4ft away, perhaps assuming that, if Romeo considered me safe, then maybe she could, too. Romeo reached for the peanut and Juliet moved closer as if to say, "Hey, what about me?" Slowly I reached back into my bag, pulled out another peanut and tossed it to a couple of feet in front of Juliet. She reached it while Romeo stood his ground.

There was now no turning back; I must see if Romeo would eat from my hand. I extended it, a peanut resting in my palm. Romeo moved closer, staying sideways to me. He looked at the peanut, then at me, then back at the peanut. As he did so, Juliet moved closer but would not compete with Romeo. After a while I realized that Romeo was not going to take the peanut from my palm and so I slowly retracted my arm, placed the peanut between my index and middle finger and stretched it out again. Romeo was now about six inches from my extended fingers, and I stretched them some more by leaning my body toward Romeo, and then, still sideways, he took it from my fingers! Hooray! Victory!

Now I turned my attention to Juliet, again extended my fingers, with another lodged peanut, in her direction. She moved closer but I dropped the peanut, and she took it with the now standard sideways stance. She retreated to about 3ft, as did Romeo. Together we made a perfect equilateral triangle.

Then I shifted my weight and, in so doing, moved my right foot about six or seven inches towards the birds. They immediately took off in opposite directions before circling back and flying away together down into the canyon. For a few minutes I sat and waited, but they were gone.

I chuckled to myself, and only then did I put two and two together—the birds had turned sideways to me, not so they could keep an eye on me, but so that, if I threatened them and they had to take off, they would not be flying straight at me—they needed an escape route.

5. Grapevine's Stone Time

I got an early start the next day, choosing a good drink of water rather than setting up the stove, and using my flashlight to find my way in the early morning gloom. I was cold again, but only because of the early hour, and I knew that once on the trail I would soon be warm. Even though it was still March, once the sun rose high enough to reach me, the day would quickly heat up. It was time to make some distance along the trail, firstly across the first two Cremation drainages, which I already knew.

I made it down and up both drainages, finding their cairns and happy to see the small one I had created the day before. By the time I reached the third drainage, the first rays of sun were hitting the area. The east drainage water was still high, maybe ten inches deep, but I was ready for the crossing. I took off my hiking shoes and put on Tevas. I hung my hiking shoes around my neck and cautiously started out into the water, taking small steps to keep my balance in the current. Most of the stones on the bottom were small, so it was a relatively stable walking surface.

I reached the other side without difficulty, got back into my hiking shoes, and hit the trail, turning north to get around the 5,000ft Pattie Butte. According to the author and photographer John Annerino (1949–), the width of the three Cremation drainages was 0.82 mile, or about 1 mile from Cave Rock. From there I had 3.09 miles to go before Lonetree and then a further 2.88 miles on to Boulder Creek—approximately 7 miles from start to finish. In those days, that was about my limit for a normal day, especially if I was hoping to find my next campsite at around noon. But I had a choice: I could stop at Boulder or go on to Grapevine. I would decide once I reached Boulder, letting my body dictate. According to the Heart Map, there were no exposed sections of trail all the way from Boulder to Grapevine.

The walk around Pattie Butte was relatively flat and the Tonto Plateau was alive with the beautiful yellow blooms of the blackbrush, a member of the rose family. On the east side of the butte the trail bent south to meet the trail that crossed Lonetree Canyon. Lonetree is a small side canyon, about the length of Cremation but neither as wide, nor as deep. As I approached the creek crossing, it looked like the pool of water at the bottom of the little waterfall would have enough water for a sponge bath, but Cremation has plenty of water, as does Grapevine, so I figured I could bathe anywhere. Despite the water, Lonetree was without green vegetation, and I was looking forward to finding some at Grapevine. So, I stopped just long enough to cup my hands and splash my face and neck, and then marched on to Boulder.

Now the trail had to skirt Newton Butte, 5,928ft at its highest. A northern part of the butte peaks at 4,943ft, which forces the trail back toward the Inner Gorge's rim at a mere 3,753ft and then back north and around a very small un-named side canyon, and finally to the trail crossover of Boulder Creek. When I arrived at the point next to the Inner Gorge, I stopped, took off my backpack, and inched my way towards the edge of the drop-off. From there I could see both Zoroaster Canyon and Clear Creek Canyon, and below me the Fifty-Three Mile Rapids on the Colorado. I took a few minutes to gaze across at the North Side, standing still as I did so. Number one rule: "Don't look out while walking."

I returned to my backpack, loaded up, and continued on to a relatively flat trail, past the unnamed side canyon, and across the Plateau. After two further drainages, I reached the Boulder Creek cross-over. The trail skirted Boulder's west side and it was clear that only the east side offered any campsite and, even there, it was rather rocky. I took off my pack and looked around. There were spaces between the exposed large boulders, with grass coming up from soil, but I found only one place big enough for my tent. I was on the side of Lyell Butte (at 5,367ft only just below Newton Butte) and there was no flat ground. It was almost noon and I had to make my choice. I could go on to Grapevine (a further 5.8 miles) or stay here and make the best of the uneven ground. There was water here, but not as much as I would find at Grapevine, and if I reached Grapevine that day, I would have more time to explore it and Cottonwood beyond. If I did that, I reasoned, I could camp at Boulder on the way back, on the one flat grassy site that I had seen, and maybe also even stop at Lonetree and enjoy that little waterfall. I ate lunch as I contemplated and, by the time I had finished, rested, and energized, I had decided: for once I would break my own rule of spending the afternoon at a good site and, instead, would push on to Grapevine. "Get ready for me, Grapevine," I said out loud, but the buttes, majestic in their beauty, made no reply. Nevertheless, I felt better having decided to push myself another 5-plus miles to a good campsite. I needed to lie on a rock and hear water rushing by me.

As I walked, I thought about how totally isolated I was and thus, how vulnerable. I got in the habit of checking for rattlesnakes with my hiking pole wherever I walked or sat. Once the sun was fully out, the snakes will desert the trail, but if you accidentally disturb their holes or sheltering places between the rocks, they will strike. I was always listening for the warning rattle, but I had learned from experience that they don't always sound the alarm, especially in the morning when they are still half frozen. One day, when fishing in the High Sierras, I had stepped onto a rock and was reaching for the next, when a very large diamond-back rattler moved suddenly between the rocks, probably preparing to strike. I pulled my leg back quickly and retreated to safety. A snake bite can kill you and, when alone, it pays to understand "the enemies" lurking around you in the wilderness.

Once more I checked my Heart Map, looking for exposure on the trail. It left the east side of Boulder and climbed up and east. As the Colorado River reaches the distant foot of Lyell Butte (5,367ft), it turns east, goes around another no-name side canyon of the Inner Gorge, and then snakes north until it reaches the very edge of the Inner Gorge. On the map, that area is cream colored, meaning it is as flat as the Tonto Plateau gets.

I traversed the long exposure section of the trail without problem, rested a little, and then continued. The trail began its in and out weaving across the countless little drainages of the west side of Grapevine, went around two fairly large side canyons, and then I noticed that the canyon's floor, its stream bed, was rising up to me—I was approaching the crossing. Grapevine is the only permanently flowing creek in this area, so I expected the crossing to be dry, or nearly so. Indeed, as it turned out, only one of Cremation's drainages was wet that day. As I approached the 3,500ft contour of the canyon's rim, the trail swung southwest and crossed the first drainage. There was no campsite, so I paused, drank from my canteen, ate some trail mix, and moved on. In a short while I came to the second drainage. As I looked at the trail on the map, I fancied the double crossing looked much like a woman's high-heel shoe, and it occurred to me that this high-heel twisting may well have reminded someone of a twisting grapevine, and it was for that, rather than any fruit-bearing vegetation, that this side canyon was named "Grapevine."

At last, I reached the main creek and, with delight, heard the sound of flowing water. I had arrived at the base of Horseshoe Mesa and Cottonwood Creek. There was a perfect camping area beside the creek, and it was with utter joy that I plunked down my backpack and drank what was left of the water in my canteen. There was no one in sight; I was totally alone.

It must have been about 4:00 p.m. and, knowing that I was close to the Grandview Trail that comes from the rim and that there was still time for others to show up before dark, I decided to stake my claim and pitch my tent beside the creek. Then, I took out my stove and pot, picked up my sleeping mattress and headed down to the creek in search of a warm dry rock on which to stretch out and rest my weary body—I was in need of some "stone time."

I found a large flat stone, about 20ft by 30ft, worn smooth by centuries of rushing water. I looked around in all directions, including up to the west rim of the canyon, and saw absolutely no one. The silence was broken only by the running water. The sun was now in the west, warming my body.

A slight breeze blew, and I luxuriated in the warmth coming up from the rock. Exhaustion was replaced by a simple joy of living and, despite the warning voice in the back of my mind reminding me of the dangers of the sun's effects on my fair skin, the Grand Canyon filled and overwhelmed my heart.

The subtitle of this book is: "The Psyche of Water and Stone." What symbols do these two substances evoke? Such a direct question is hard to answer without delving into the history of humankind's relationship with these two objects. The first philosopher of sorts, the pre-Socratic Thales of Miletus, proclaimed that the primordial element is water: "All is water," he said. Probably he thought of the oceans that surround the continents, and then of the water that falls from the sky, the rain, and if one digs down through the earth, one will reach water from "the water table." If there is water below and above and around, surely Thales had a point, and while he did not know it, physiologists tell us that more than 90% of the human body is water. It is obvious to me that the elements—earth, air, fire, and water—are symbols, not signs indicating what we now think of as physical elements.

Philosophy is the love of wisdom, while science gives us knowledge of the natural world, including that of the human body and brain. These two forms of thinking are separate mental realms, and they are incommensurable.

We live in the age of positivism, with, of course, no epistemological sophistication. Philosophy outranks positivism because the latter is a faulty philosophy of science, since positivism's method of finding truth—that of experiments backed by radical empiricism—cannot verify its own belief that science is the only way to truth. As Plato's "Seventh Letter" says, there is no substitute to "repeated being with, and living with, the matter itself," since "it is brought to birth in the soul suddenly."

Bergson thought of *élan vital* as "a kind of vital impetus, which explains evolution in a less mechanical and more lively manner, as well as accounting for the creative impulse of mankind," according to *Wikipedia*. This is of no help, for what is a "vital impetus"? Vital means "necessary for life," and "impetus" means either (a) "the property possessed by a moving body in virtue of its mass and its motion," or (b) "stimulation or encouragement resulting in increased activity." (These definitions from *Webster's Collegiate Dictionary* are double in nature, one for each side, as it were, of the fundamental incommensurable dichotomy.) The French *élan* translates as "vigorous spirit or enthusiasm"—such definition sounding very much like the Latin term, *anima*, as in the he or she that is animated by *eros*.

I will simplify: *élan* means being really alive, rather than merely one of the many who are like the walking dead. Philosophy belongs in the humanities; those who try to put it within the sciences are simply aping the sciences.

And so, we return to the question: What does water symbolize?

29

Perhaps, *élan vital*. The psyche energy, that which makes us human. The flow of water (animation) over stone (the foundation of inner life) evokes the human psyche's meaningfulness. Hence, the sub-title of this book.

Thoreau warned that when you come to die, you must have fully lived. He built his hut looking out over the waters of Walden Pond; I built a house in New Hampshire on the bank of cascading water-falls. Now I live with a view of the Atlantic Ocean crashing on the rocks of Loblobby Cove. I cannot live without water, without flow; not the water we find in a bottle, but the "water of the inner life." In viewing my cascading water, I arrive at the notion that water follows the contour of the stone beneath it, while very slowly shaping that same stone, and the human psyche must do the same, following nature, whatever it dishes out, following its contours.

And what of stone? What does it symbolize? What comes to mind is the alchemists' goal to make "the philosopher's stone." Carl Jung wrote in *Psychology and Alchemy*:

> There are people, of course, who think it unscientific to take anything seriously; they do not want their intellectual playground disturbed by graver considerations. But the doctor who fails to take account of man's feeling for values commits a serious blunder, and if he tries to correct the mysterious and well-nigh inscrutable workings of nature with his so-called scientific attitude, he is merely putting his shallow sophistry in place of nature's healing processes. Let us take the wisdom of the old alchemists to heart: *Nateuralissimum et perfectissimum opus est generare tale quale ipsum est*. [The most natural and perfect work is to generate its like.]
>
> —Carl Jung, *Psychology and Alchemy*, Vol 12,
> *The Collected Works of C.G. Jung* (Princeton University Press, 1968.)

And, Jung continues, "...there is certain incommensurability between the mystery of existence and human understanding." Later in the same work, Jung gives a concise definition of alchemy:

It should now be sufficiently clear that from its earliest days alchemy had a double face: on the one hand the practical chemical work in the laboratory, on the other a psychological process, in part consciously psychic, in part unconsciously projected and seen in the various transformations of matter.

The philosopher's stone, physically, is the conscious work of the alchemist: the stone is no ordinary one, but rather one with a philosophical significance. Jung calls the psychological process of alchemy—that part of the alchemist's work that is unconscious— "individuation," and the philosopher's stone is one of the symbols for the achievement of individuation. Why stone? My intuition tells me that "stone" represents strength, that which one can trust. Stone is solid, for the most part, and solid is a term we use for people with strength, as in "solid character." Early in *Psychology and Alchemy*, Jung writes:

Occasionally one meets such patients again after several years and hears the often highly remarkable account of their subsequent development. It was experiences of this kind which first confirmed me in my belief that there is in the psyche a process that seeks its own goal independently of external factors, and which freed me from the worrying feeling that I myself might be the sole cause of an unreal—and perhaps unnatural—process in the psyche of the patient.

The stone is the psychic foundation, over which must flow the water of animated feeling and intuition. Water follows the contours of stone, welling up the potholes (complexes) with a healing force. The Grand Canyon, **perhaps more than any other place on this globe, demonstrates the power of water on stone.**

It is not enough to engage in "soul making," which many Jungians believe in, for nature within (the Subjective) must participate in the process and connect with nature without, thus expressing the "Objective Psyche." In other words, there is an "outer" dimension within the inner psyche as well as an "inner" dimension within the outer nature. The merging of these two—psyche and nature—produces a quaternity, the two inner dimensions meeting their opposites, the two outer dimensions. Under this dynamic, individuation takes place, an inner quaternity, a solid wholeness symbolized by the number four.

In my view, no other psychology deals with this complex mystery, and hence, only depth psychology can explain why the confrontation with nature is necessary for the psyche's individuation. I do not consider Sigmund Freud (1856–1939) to be a depth psychologist, even though Jung learned from him, while also insisting that Freud needed an analysis. Freud was a positivist who believed that psychoanalysis is a science, whereas Jung fully embraced the history (including esotericism) of the humanities. This is why psychoanalysts need an M.D. degree and Jungians don't. Jungians use their nature to heal, whereas M.D.s use their scientific credentials. Thus, Jungians talk to you and bring out your feelings and notions, whereas doctors prescribe medication after studying the data derived from your blood analysis. The Platonic tradition uses the term "world soul," and Jung follows it with the title of his "nature writings." (See, *The Earth Has a Soul*, edited by Meredith Sabini; North Atlantic Books, Berkeley, California, 2002.)

My "stone time" by the side of Grapevine Creek was key to allowing my mind to revert to its natural state; my psyche of stone closed the gap between myself and the stone that was supporting my body.

I dressed and retreated a little way downstream, fired up the camp stove and pumped some water for the next day's trek to Cottonwood. It would be the end of my 18-mile hike on the Tonto East trail. Still alone, I went to bed even earlier than my habit, for my long trek from Cremation to Grapevine had tired me. For three days I had seen no one. The heavenly noise of the creek passing by my site put me to sleep within minutes. Tomorrow I would hike to Cottonwood, on the edge off and below Horseshoe Mesa. Tomorrow, perhaps, I would meet a fellow traveler.

6. Scout Leader Dynamics

The individual forming part of a group acquires, solely from numerical considerations, a sentiment of invincible power which allows him to yield to instincts which, had he been alone, he would perforce have kept under restraint. A group being anonymous and in consequence irresponsible, the sentiment of responsibility which always controls individuals disappears entirely.

—Sigmund Freud, *Group Psychology and the Analysis of the Ego*
(Bantam Books, 1960)

I awoke to the "talking" of the creek and wondered what time it was. I pushed the button on my watch—4:00 a.m. It was still not quite light, but I was astonished to find that I had slept for nine hours. I stretched, listened, and then stuck my head out through the mesh just enough to look around without leaving my sleeping bag. Once again there was no evidence of anyone else being in the vicinity.

The sun was soon hitting the campsite and I crawled out of my tent. To my surprise, I discovered that it had rained overnight. Fortunately, I always bring my backpack into the tent to avoid the pack rats, so nothing but the fly of the tent was wet.

Cottonwood was not far away—3.43 miles according to Annerino—so I decided to enjoy some breakfast before heading out, and then, to walk around a little while my tent fly dried out in the morning air. As I walked, I reflected on the pros and cons of Grapevine—joyous flowing water and smooth flat rocks, but only one tree and no vines or other greenery.

The trail rose on the east side of Grapevine, going north before turning east toward Cottonwood. On the Park's topo map, I had noticed a spring just after the trail climbs away from Grapevine's rim and decided that, while I still had a good supply of water, I might nevertheless stop there to enjoy the greenery. But when I reached the spot, it was to find that the "spring" was nothing more than a little water seep and a few small bushes. However, the climb was not bad and after a while I stopped at a large rock on the right side of the trail, with a little amphitheater just beyond it. I stared at the trail as it crossed this curved amphitheater. About 20ft in, the trail narrowed to just a foot wide and then to a little less than half that—just enough space to place one foot in front of the other. Furthermore, where the trail was at its narrowest, the amphitheater was soaking wet! I could not believe it. None of my guidebooks had warned me of this feature.

I sat down on the large rock, slipped out of my pack, and took another look. The distance across the amphitheater was only about 40ft, but above and, perhaps more importantly, below the trail, there was nothing but a steep slope covered in small gravel all the way to the drop off—if I were to slip, there was nothing to stop me from going over the edge, and nothing to take hold of. I have never seen anything as scary as this little piece of trail. If only it were dry! I was worried not only about slipping, but also of causing a cave-in. There had to be an alternative. I didn't want to give up on Cottonwood—where, I had been told, there were beautiful trees and a waterfall—but nor was I quite ready to die in the pursuit!

I went back along the trail about 10ft to see if there was another way. But with no climbing gear to take me safely above the amphitheater, it seemed a lost cause. Perhaps, after all, I would have to turn back.

Then, to my utter surprise, I heard something like a human sound. I looked back down the trail and saw no one—clearly the isolation was getting to me. Then I heard it again and, there, about 50ft below me, I saw a hat coming up the trail. I waited.

A large man in a cowboy hat moved into view. He was accompanied by several boys walking behind him. As they drew closer, they separated into one man and seven or eight boys.

"Howdy," said the man.

"How are the boys doing?" I asked.

"We came down the Kaibab and slept over at Boulder and are now going up to the rim via Grandview," he replied.

I drew his attention to the hazardous trail ahead and said that the boys looked tired and very hot.

He glanced back at his charges and said to me, "We'll rest when we get to the Grandview at the Mesa, and the boys can change their wet tee shirts for dry ones and drink lots of water."

I again pointed out that the trail just ahead was wet, that there was lot of exposure and a very thin trail for maybe 10ft or so.

He looked to where I was pointing and said, "That's nothing, my boys will handle that."

I asked if they were Boy Scouts, and the man said yes, he was leading them and had been "doing this for years now." Then, after taking a breath, he said, "I've toughened them up on this trip."

I felt like responding that even the tough can fall under circumstances such as this, but decided to keep my mouth shut… clearly this guy was going on, regardless.

I thought, *There's perhaps a 10% chance that one of the kids, or more than one, might fall to his death: is that worth the Boy Scout toughening process?*

By now the leader was way ahead of the boys, striding out into the amphitheater. Without hesitation, the boys followed him. I shook my head in disbelief; apparently none of them had an inkling of the danger they were in.

I decided to follow, but first would shift my pack's weight to the uphill, or inner side of the trail. I was opening my pack to make the necessary adjustments, when I saw another boy coming towards me. Quite chubby, very red in the face and sweating a good deal, he was obviously the laggard of the group. He was wearing tennis shoes.

I stopped him as he passed me and told him to be careful because the trail ahead was very wet and very narrow. I couldn't tell him not to cross, because he was part of the troop and not my responsibility, nor did I want to help him across, because that would probably make him nervous and might endanger him more than just letting him walk on as if there were no danger. But, if he slipped off the trail or it gave way, I could stick out my Leki pole and hope that he would grab it.

I told him again to take it easy and be careful. He nodded and stepped out into the amphitheater. I watched him walk, oblivious to the danger, and go on his way. I heaved a sigh of relief and then wondered: If I did as the boy did, would that damn trail give way on me, the guy who takes every precaution, while the boy, all the boys, and that irresponsible leader, were saved from extinction? I weighed far more than the boys, but was probably a fair bit lighter than their leader. I shifted the weight to the inside, took out my second pole, extended it only part way, made sure the longer one was on the outside, and headed out, practicing my "no crossing of legs walk"—left foot ahead, right foot up next to its middle, then left ahead, repeat. Thus, I always had one foot fully on the ground. The trail held true, and I made it across, sat down again and took deep breaths. Perhaps I had been over-cautious, but, I decided, better cautious than foolhardy.

The rest of the trail was easy, no exposure and no alternative trails to confuse me. Soon it turned south, until it reached a side drainage to the Cottonwood Creek. There it looped, went north and then back to south where the map indicated another spring. I continued up the trail and before long came to the Cottonwood grove of large trees, very similar to those at Indian Garden. There was a small waterfall, about 5ft or so in drop, with a little pool below—not big enough to bathe in, but sufficient to pump drinking water from. Since I was below the Mesa where many people camp, I decided to boil my water when I reloaded my canteens. I set up my tent as close to the waterfall as reasonable and cupped water in my hands to cool my head and face. I was alone again, alone in a beautiful hole. Cottonwood was surely one of the best sites on the trip—what more could an inner journey ask for than a waterfall and massive trees? But the best was yet to come!

After spending the rest of the day walking around the campsite and, finding no one, I watched the waterfall and lay out next to it, looking up and through the massive trees. I went to bed early, had a good sleep, and awoke at daylight. I broke camp and climbed back onto the trail, but when I reached the crossing of the Tonto East trail, I decided to ignore it and, instead, took the Grandview Trail to see what I could see. A mile or so farther on I found a yucca stalk lying over the trail. Then I came upon more and more. I broke one off and stowed it in my pack—I would keep it as a memento of the canyon. It made it back with me to the East Coast, and today stands next to my desk in the study—a daily remembrance of my beloved Grand Canyon.

7. A Heavenly Woman

I went back down the trail to the Tonto and headed west. It was time to head back. I crossed the exposed little amphitheater without trouble—for the ground was totally dry now—made it back to the Grapevine site, ate some breakfast, and climbed back out the west side of Cremation, stopping at the overlook of the Grapevine Rapids to have a snack before going on to Boulder. I pitched my tent in the one spot between the rocks large enough to accommodate it, and a few minutes later was sitting on a stone close to Boulder Creek. I was truly relaxed: the trail back from Boulder Creek to Cremation and the Cave Rock was relatively straight. I would be walking through all the yellow flowers of the Blackbrush and, when I reached Cremation river, it would surely be half the size it had been when I crossed it last. The rest of the day could be given over to stone time.

Then—disaster!—I discovered I was running low on food. I had only one dinner left, and I needed two—one for Boulder and one for Cremation. I realized now that my two-day rest had not been according to plan and that I should have reduced my rations in both those dinners so that I would have enough to stretch for an extra meal. I would have to skip dinner and eat a power bar and the rest of the trail mix instead. I would chalk it up as another mistake to add to my list of lessons learned. I went back to my stone time and stayed there until the sun was low in the west and the day began to cool off.

Some time later, I was aware of a noise that sounded human. At first, I thought that, perhaps, I had imagined it, but in a few moments I saw a very attractive woman with a large backpack coming across the creek in my direction. I stood up and saw that she was being followed by five or six men, all with big packs. Boulder is in the Grand Canyon's BH9 section, which is designated as "Primitive." The rule is that only one party may be present at a campsite, and a solo hiker is considered a "party." A party can be from one to eight people—such as the scout party I had met—while a group is nine to sixteen. I hoped this party would go on to Grapevine when they saw me—I certainly wasn't ready for such social contact. I was off the trail about 20ft or so, so imagined that they would just pass on by.

But, instead, the woman headed straight to me, smiling.

I said, "Howdy," establishing with one word that I was a westerner and not one of those questionable easterners.

She commented that I had the best tent site and said, "Good for you," before asking where I was coming from. I explained my out-and-back trip, and she asked, "Are you all alone?"

I nodded.

Then she said something like, "I didn't expect someone here at Boulder, but my group is too tired to go on to Grapevine. I know that you have a right to camp at Boulder by yourself and that the rules mean we should go on to Grapevine."

I asked her if she was the leader of this party. She introduced herself and explained that she led groups as part of the Grand Canyon Institute. I explained to her that I had been seeking aloneness on this trip, since my wife could not come because of her job as a teacher, while I was on spring break from my university.

She asked me what and where I taught, and I told her, "The

Philosophy of Nature" and "Philosophy of Native American Religion" at Suffolk University in Boston.

By now I was assuming she would be staying put—she clearly did not want to go on to Grapevine at this late hour, and here she was, chatting with some guy from Boston, a philosophy professor no less, who was into nature and Native Americans... *at worst he was likely harmless, at best he might be interesting.*

And then I realized we could make a deal. She wanted to stay put and I needed food.

"We have plenty of food, far more than we need," she smiled again.

I smiled back. "If you can find enough room for all of you somewhere above my tent, I will trade my solo status for some of your food. But I have been alone for five days and nights, so you will have to forgive me if I'm a little rusty in talking to other humans."

Again, she smiled and then quickly laughed and said, "How does macaroni and cheese, with cuts of sausage sound? All you can eat, and you can join us for breakfast as well as dinner."

Which is how I met my "Heavenly Woman." I ate as much as I could at dinner and then she asked me how it was that a philosopher would teach about Nature and Native Americans. Surely, philosophy was "very abstract"?

I explained as best as I could, insisting that the tradition of philosophy had gotten off the necessary tract since Plato, and that I was trying to get it back on track. That led to more questions, and soon I had to excuse myself and get to bed. I was in my fifties, I explained, and the "best meal I have had bar none in the Grand Canyon" had made me sleepy.

I thanked them for dinner and asked what time breakfast was. The woman smiled and said, "You're the guest, whenever you're ready, just give a shout if we are not up, and we will join you and whip up breakfast. Do you like pancakes with fruit?" They even had Vermont maple syrup! Perhaps my wife and I needed to join one of these group trips in the future—spreading the burden of supplies sounded like heaven to me.

Breakfast the next morning was excessive, but I ate my fill once more. All of us were on the trail somewhat early, and we said our goodbyes as I turned for Cremation and they set off for Grape-vine. I was headed for Cave Rock and thence for the final ascent on the South Kaibab Trail, and I had enough food to keep me going through it all. What a lucky guy!

8. Cremation Flats and a Little Grass

Us nature mystics got to stick together.

—Edward Abbey, *A Voice Crying in the Wilderness: Notes From a Secret Journal* (St. Martin's Griffin, 1989)

I was back at Cave Rock. It felt like coming home. But I decided to walk on up the slope and check out the area I called the Flats. Since the Flats were as close to the Kaibab Trail as I could get on level ground, I had decided to camp there my last night. As much as I liked Cave Rock—indeed it had saved my life that first night—some impulse told me I should experience the Flats as well. From there I had a view all the way to the edge of the Inner Gorge. I liked the idea of being able to see Zoroaster Temple, and I wanted to walk down the drainage to the north of the Flat's campsite to peek over the edge and into the Inner Gorge. Besides, it would put me closer to the South Kaibab Trail for my final ascent.

I sat down on one of the rocks, studied my Heart Map, and picked out Zoroaster Temple, 7,131ft, with its magnificent, sculptured "legs" splaying out in all directions, as if to support the monolith. Between the campsite and the Inner Gorge stood a 700ft-high hill, but it did not block the view of the towering Zoroaster.

The name "Zoroaster" is an English corruption of the Persian name, "Zarathustra," and was used by Nietzsche for his alter ego, his hero once human nature returned to its natural glory. Zarathustra's namesake was the founder of Zoroastrianism, a dualistic religion of two spiritual entities, one good, one evil. As I stared at the great Zoroaster, I was reminded of Nietzsche's book, *Beyond Good and Evil* (A Gateway Edition, Henry Regnery Co., 1955), and the overlooked version of his "thought of thoughts," that of eternal return. After giving up the notion of life after death, Nietzsche created a substitute, better than the religious notion of a theistic God who rewards us for our good deeds and punishes our bad deeds with hell. Leading up to his "thought of thoughts," Nietzsche insists that "the Father" in God is thoroughly refuted, likewise the "judge" and the "rewarder." Also, his "free will—he does not hear us, and even if he heard us, he could not help." Then Nietzsche speaks of "the great ladder of religious cruelty," the rungs of which ask for the entire sacrifice of oneself to God. This is the history of religious Gnosticism, which overtook Judaeo-Christianity, and which features anti-nominalism and sado-masochism, the "sacrifice of God for nothingness," as well as the opposite practice of no sex, a life of celibacy and austerity. These two extremes, masochism and sadism, are caught up in what Jung calls *enantiodromia*, the conversion of one into its opposite, e.g., from positivism to gnosticism.

Contrary to the teachings of Walter Kaufmann (1921–1980) and Martin Heidegger (1889–1976), the "eternal return" is not cosmological but entirely *psychological*. Nietzsche has not "left" religion, not at all: "It seems to me," he wrote, "that the religious instinct is growing powerfully but is rejecting theistic gratification with deep distrust."

The eternal return is part of Nietzsche's new religion; his goal is to formulate a "religion of the earth":

> Whoever has really looked at the most world-negating of all possible ways of thinking with Asiatic and ultra-Asiatic eyes—truly beyond good and evil and no longer, like Buddha and Schopenhauer, under the spell and illusion of morality—such a man has perhaps had his eyes opened, even without having wanted it, to the opposite ideal, the ideal

of the truly exuberant, alive, and world-affirming man who does not merely resign himself to and learn to get along with all that was and is, but who wants everything *as it was and returns*, back forever and ever, insatiably calling *de capo*, not only to himself but to the whole spectacle and performance, and not only to the performance but basically to that which necessitates and needs the performance because it forever and ever necessitates and needs itself! …Perhaps some day the solemn concepts about which we struggled and suffered most, the concepts "God" and "sin," will appear no more important to us than a child's toy or a child's grief appears to an old man. And then perhaps the "old man," mankind, will need another toy and another grief—still enough of a child himself, forever and ever a child!

—Friedrich Nietzsche, *Beyond Good and Evil*
(Penguin Publishing Group, 1990)

Here Nietzsche is speaking of "the child within," that which makes mankind's "world grow deeper." He is speaking of the inner journey, that which embraces all that came before, and the *de capo* is a call to start over again, to repeat one's life in the process that the Greeks called *anamnesis*. All of which is exactly what I was doing while sitting on that rock and looking at Zoroaster's Temple. To relive one's life in thought is to pull one's experiences into a unity, a wholeness, as in the Greek word "pan." The structure of *logos*, of meaning, is that which the eternal return creates *in this world*. Anamnesis is not cosmology, projected outward from the human psyche, but psychology, drawn inward, the crucial process of living the inner journey.

That late afternoon I sensed what Jung called a "synchronicity," that is, a psychically meaningful coincidence, a connection between two things that is perceived by the psyche and is not a causal (outward) connection, but rather an inward *meaningful connection*. I was looking at Zoroaster Temple and noticed that its top is in the shape of a pyramid, and from my viewing place, Cremation Flats, I saw only one triangular face of the whole pyramid.

While looking at that triangle I immediately remembered when my wife and I travelled to Sils Maria—a small Swiss village in the Upper Engadine, a high alpine region whose valley floor is at 6,000ft—to visit The Nietzsche House, an old boarding house in which Nietzsche wrote the beginnings of his Zarathustra book. The major idea of the book is that of the *wish* for eternal return, and, amazingly, the idea occurred to Nietzsche when he was sitting on the shores of Lake Silvaplana with his back *to a pyramidal block of stone*, not unlike Zoroaster Temple's triangle when seen across the Inner Gorge.

There were no other large blocks of stone on that lakeside to compete with the one pyramidal stone— about 5–6ft high. I spent time, as Nietzsche did, with my back resting on that rock's side, looking out over the beautiful lake. Out of curiosity, I climbed to a waterfall behind the stone. Most of the water from the fall's stream went into the lake to my right, but a small amount broke off and flowed to my left. There was no sign that the stones around the waterfall had broken off and fallen through the trees to the lakeshore. And yet that must have been the origin of the triangular stone against which Nietzsche leaned and experienced a deep-nature absorption.

Synchronicity connected my thoughts of the eternal return while sitting alone on Cremation Flats. The triangular images of Zoroaster and Nietzsche's rock had unleashed my mind and I considered the enigmas that Nietzsche offered: the religion beyond religion, the "religion of the earth," as he called it; a religion of soul, psyche, rather than "spirit," and the desire for a repetition of one's life out of pure joy for what it was.

"Religion" means to be fixed at a psychological center, to be orientated (Eliade), to find "ultimate concern" (Tillich). I bet that Nietzsche, while sitting against his rock, was watching the sunlight play on the lake water and became consumed by the "eternal return," the notion that life is dearest only when one can *wish* to live it again. Could I *wish* to relive all my Grand Canyon experiences?

I don't pretend to think that whoever named Zoroaster Temple did so because of Nietzsche and his book, but Zarathustra Canyon lies just to the east of Zoroaster Temple, so there is another possible synchronicity concerning the name.

In *Thus Spake Zarathustra*, Nietzsche starts with Zarathustra's Prologue, "his" Speeches, the first of which is "The Three Metamorphoses." I believe that these three metamorphoses are pertinent to our inner journey: "I tell you how the spirit becomes a camel; and the camel, a lion, and the lion, finally, a child." Nietzsche's "child" is the Inner Child, the secret reward of the old man who isn't looking for anything because his "world grows deeper." It seems to me that such astonishing synchronicity, where everything seems to fit together and to have meaningful connection, gives us layers of inner depth. To experience such synchronistic depths is life relived.

Pandora was the goddess who was given a jar (or box) and was told not to look in it, but she did so and out flew all the evils in the world. Pandora's Box symbolizes the human psyche, and to take off the lid is symbolically to project all that is in the psyche outward, causing evil, rather than to live with one's inner life. Pandora's fault was not curiosity but outward projection; evil is inevitable when one lives without any notion or connection to his or her soul, thereby projecting outward, onto others. Today's world is full of scapegoating, blaming others for our faults. I call it "the 180-degree rule"— blaming others for what is coming from oneself. It is what makes the world seem "upside down" (see: Melanie Phillips' *The World Turned Upside Down: The Global Battle Over God, Truth, and Power* [Encounter Books, 2010]).

Having watched the sun cast its shadows on the canyon's walls— a myriad of shadows and bright sunlight slowly giving way to darkness—I put up my tent and laid out my sleeping bag, then ate my last dinner. As usual, I went to bed at the beginning of the canyon's night. I was planning a daybreak start up South Kaibab Trail next morning—it is important to get through the cobblestone switchbacks before the sun warms the trail below Skeleton Point. I had plenty of water left, and had all day to walk out, but the thought of leaving Cremation made me sad. Overall, I said to myself, I had had a good hike. I couldn't deny that Cremation was special.

I reflected on my journey. It had been a successful trip, made a little more pleasant because of the absence of other hikers—except for the Boy Scouts and the group of men guided by that heavenly angel. I had to admit that I had come close to running out of food and had almost died on my descent, but then, as now, I had been lucky.

However, I also had to admit that it had not produced the moment of deep-nature absorption and ecstasy that I had hoped for, and while the ravens had been interesting, they were not a part of my inner journey. I decided to light my small candles as a final gesture before falling to sleep, so I dug them out, and crawled into my sleeping bag, with the tent and bag facing east so I could see the dawning light of tomorrow from my bag. I put the three candles on the dirt, lit them, then watched their flickering light as I rested and prepared for sleep. The candles were only a half inch thick, and one by one they burned up their wicks. The moon had come up and the ground around me was bathed in a pool of moonlight. It was a lovely night, not at all cool, and the moonlight warmed my heart so that I did not feel ready to sleep. In fact, a strong emotion began to invade me—one of great gratitude for this canyon and my experiences.

In a few minutes, I noticed that the moonlight was shining on a few bits of grass. I was surprised because the Cremation Flats seemed to have no vegetation, especially at this end—here, there was nothing more than dark, packed earth, almost like pavement. A light wind moved the grass and it seemed to dance before me— what a hard time it must have had, making its way up and through that barren soil! According to my trail notes, my mind turned again to Nietzsche. I wondered if he had coined his famous phrase, "the will to power," after seeing the phenomenon of plants growing up through every crack in the modern "concrete" of our world. I was overcome with my gratitude for my life, good and bad, to the point of my eyes watering.

Then it happened, as if my brain had switched onto another level, or perhaps took a short break from my body. Of course, I immediately knew what was happening, an ecstasy, this time induced by a few blades of grass. I thought of Walt Whitman's *Leaves of Grass*, where "grass" serves as a metaphor for all of nature. The ecstasy was evoked by a combination of light and meaningful connections flooding my mind. A joy and gratitude for my life, for the canyon, for my luck, for all of life, overwhelmed me. It lasted about fifteen minutes, I think, although it is difficult to estimate, since ecstasy also seems to create a sense of "time stood still." My memory of it seems to be of a full ecstasy, of gratitude for life, and a deep sense of joy.

And so, the canyon had given me my wished-for ecstasy experience. Somehow, suddenly and unexpectedly, the trip's goal had been reached. Heraclitus was right: the psyche has no limits, outside of time and coming "out of nowhere."

In the Fourth Part of *Thus Spoke Zarathustra*, Nietzsche says:

> Have you ever said Yes to a single joy? O my friends, then you said Yes to *all* woe. All things are entangled, ensnared, enamored; if ever you wanted one thing twice, if ever you said, "You please me, happiness! Abide, moment!" then you wanted *all* back.

Indeed, to "want" or to "will," as in Nietzsche's "will to power," his essential theme throughout his life, is the only way to experience immortality or "eternity." We die at death, a personal extinction, the releasing of our place in the world for others to use. But after a full life, death is like the end of a play or book. With no ending there is no book or play, nor so much wisdom and joy. Wanting all of it back, the good and the bad, means the wanting, the will of return, and makes us live, in short interludes, as if we were eternal. Thoreau's imagery agrees with Nietzsche: "time is a stream I go a-fishing in." Why not the fish as inner archetypes and to fish, metaphorically, meaning to stand out of the flow of time (the stream), experiencing the eternal moments of ecstasy? Looking back, it occurs to me that my big catches were ecstasies. Yes, I could go with Nietzsche and say, "yes, YES, I wish to live it all again and again, the good with the bad, the stress with the joy. Yes, Yes, Yes. May the grass find its way up along with me, in a world full of gray."

Thoreau insisted that "heaven is under our feet, everywhere." He also said, "Surely joy is the condition of life." It is also why Nietzsche tried to create a "religion of the earth."

Of course, all heretofore religions have focused on Heaven being a release from the prison of this world, so Nietzsche or Thoreau did not offer a new religion. For them, earthly life is not a prison; the prison is that of confining oneself in only one's ego, thereby prohibiting any true ecstasy of mind without bodily addiction. Here, on my final night in Cremation, I had discovered the meaning of the "eternal return," that of consecrating all of life, its good and its bad, its "beyond good and evil."

Whether or not I returned to the Grand Canyon, my inner journey would continue, but always with a backwards glance at my canyon imagery, a smile on my face and my heart full of gratitude. The mystery of the Grand Canyon is its ability to set the stage of psychic transformation, what Kim Crumbo (1947–2021) calls "a quality experience."

Carl Jung and James Hillman (1926–2011) are the only ones I know who put the psychic depths foremost in their lives. In Jung's *Red Book* (W.W. Norton & Company, 2009) he wrote:

> Filled with human pride and blinded by the presumptuous spirit of the time, I long sought to hold that other spirit away from me. But I did not consider that the spirit of the depths from time immemorial and for all the future possesses a greater power than the spirit of this time, who changes with the generations. The spirit of the depths has subjugated all pride and arrogance to the power of judgment. He took away my

belief in science, he robbed me of the joy of explaining and ordering things, and he let devotion to the ideals of this time, die out in me. He forced me down to the last and simplest things.

That simplicity, which walked with me every step of the way along the Tonto Trail, one side canyon after the other, through archaic but beautiful campsites, one after the other, led me to what Jung called "the supreme meaning." It is the goal of Thoreau's insistence to "simplify, simplify." Jung, again in *The Red Book*, says that "the supreme meaning is the path, the way and bridge to what is to come. [...] That supreme meaning is not a meaning and not an absurdity; it is image and force in one, magnificence and force together."

At the end of my canyon's inner journey, those blades of grass dancing in the moonlight gave me an ecstasy. At the time, I sensed that it was all in my past, but now, paradoxically, it is also about my future. I have come to understand that the last stage of life involves the recollection of childhood, when all of us are "archaic humans"—giving names to imaginary figures, delighting in "magic," remembering what we dream, looking for prophecy about our future—whose egos have not yet been inflated by a culture almost entirely predisposed to science and technology. And such early life is recapitulated when moving into the last stage of life because the human psyche lusts for unity, for the pulling together of all life and seeking out its meaning, a meaning that somehow was embedded in "the soul's code" (see James Hillman's book of that title) from the very beginning of life, or perhaps even earlier.

When I was eight years old, I had a dream of God asking me whether truth is individual or a matter of public consensus. In all my studies, as well as in this book, what I address is how we humans know what we know and how we know how much we do not know. In other words, when I was young, my psyche gave me a "calling" unknown to me, until I heard the "calling" at the top of the Kaibab and Bright Angel trails. I had no intentions of writing a book about my solo trips in the Grand Canyon, but for some reason I took trail notes. I waited until I was "called" away abruptly from my teaching, my daemon whispering in my ear, "time to write your books," and I listened and agreed, retiring on the spot from my full professorship, moving inexorably toward the "ecstatic inner journey."

I close with three short sayings from two others who have walked such an inner journey, for we are never all alone in our own solitude: our mind's many dimensions insist on following the hiker's footsteps.

"Wilderness begins in the human mind."

—*A Voice Crying in the Wilderness*,
Edward Abbey (St. Martin's Griffin, 1989)

"In wildness is the preservation of the world."

—*Walking*, Henry David Thoreau
(The Atlantic, 1862)

"The highest treason, the meanest treason, is to deny the holiness of this little blue planet on which we journey through the cold void of space."

— *A Voice Crying in the Wilderness*, Edward Abbey
(St. Martin's Griffin, 1989)

But I would also look forward and quote from two of my best students: One gave me a copy of Heraclitus, fragment #45, and wrote on its front cover: "If you travel every path, you will not find the limits of the Psyche; so deep is its Logos."

The other bought me a different book and constantly reminded me of her favorite quote within it: "surely joy is the condition of life."

A hiker on the S. Kaibab Trail just before the final descent to the Tonto Platform, halfway to Phantom Ranch. Zoroaster and Brahma temples beyond. Grand Canyon N.P. NPS, Michael Quinn

CHAPTER 2

SILENCE OF THE GRAND CANYON

Side Canyons

· ·

1. What We Bring to the Grand Canyon

2. Reflections on Historic "First View"

3. The Shamanic Sipapu

In the Grand Canyon we find the locus of Nature's God. Nature does not give us "God"; nature gives us an inner experience, a mystical and ecstatic experience that, in my opinion, has ever been the source of religion. Yet, such experience can also make us philosophers—Plato, himself, founder of philosophy, had an ecstatic experience to which he referred in his Seventh Letter. Writer Edward Abbey was not religious: he joked that Jesus probably asked the headwaiter at the Last Supper for separate checks. But Abbey also proclaimed that "every man has two vocations; his own and philosophy."

This chapter will look for analogies between the Grand Canyon's unique geography and what can be called "the geography of the human psyche" (mind and soul). I call them analogies (or homologies or hierophanies) of "spiritual topographies." They lead to the inner and outer natures of us all. It is as if there were a lesson about ourselves carved out in topography, waiting in silence for our attention. The gentle incline that leads, after 17 miles, to a hole dug out of the plateau that is about 5 miles deep, is analogous to the climb of our inner journey as it emerges from ordinary experience. It is as if the two-billion-year-old rocks down by the Colorado River carry such depth of history that they must overcome our present egos and give us a notion of the transcendent life that exists deep within us.

1. What We Bring to the Grand Canyon

There is no place on Earth as enigmatic as the Grand Canyon. "Enigma" comes from the Greek *ainigma*, to speak in riddles, in symbols, oracles, mysteries, or secrets. Consciously or not, there are people who come to the Grand Canyon from all around the world looking for solutions to a variety of problems that have provoked a general dissatisfaction with modern life. But since the Grand Canyon is so mysterious, so "unreal" upon first impression, it is difficult to determine precisely how experience of it can help such visitors.

Most members of today's society believe that "where there's a will there's a way," and from childhood we try, heavy-handedly and arrogantly, to get our way by direct action. The Grand Canyon works in another way. It seems to work indirectly by metaphor. It particularly draws the aged to its mostly maintained trails. Old age is the time of metaphor and story. It is the time of bringing one's life into a unity and, hopefully, a life centered on something meaningful and purposeful—it is why Native Americans speak of "the wisdom of the elders."

One of my first impressions of the Grand Canyon, when seeing its abyss surrounded by two high plateaus, was that in some way it reconciled opposites, known in Latin as "*coincidentia oppositorum.*" As the cliché has it: "opposites attract." So it is, with certain places and persons. For example, I am a talkative guy, and the Grand Canyon is known for its "big Silence."

The National Park Service's role at the Grand Canyon is to teach the public about the geology and evolutionary history of the canyon, with side touches of prospecting history, celebrity visits, the development at the South Rim's "Village," and the role of the Grand Canyon itself in the development of the National Park System.

The National Park Service emphasizes a philosophy of humility: "The Grand Canyon is so massive and so old that it humbles us human beings." As you travel the rim and, no doubt Phantom Ranch below, you hear this everywhere: that the Grand Canyon makes us small by virtue of its enormous size and age. This notion that most Americans need a large dose of humility implies that American "exceptionalism" must be countered by the National Park Service. But, if we could expand access to the Grand Canyon and create more trails so that visitors could experience the intimate side canyons (of which there are countless examples) then surely we would experience the opposite, we would cause the psychic expansion of the souls of anyone who wished to explore the park.

As I have ventured below the rim, I have experienced a sense not of humbling but rather of gratitude: gratitude for life and for the canyon's beauty. Yes, the Grand Canyon is vast and expansive, but as I have stood within its vastness it has made me feel expanded with it. Unfortunately, most visitors do not venture into the depths of the Grand Canyon, so they experience it with a feeling of deflation, believing that the ancient history and enormous features demonstrate how insignificant they are.

As I solo backpacked in the Grand Canyon, it further became clear to me that one does not have to give up religion in order to think of the earth scientifically; one can have science as the outward journey and religion as the inner journey, if religion's baggage of premodern beliefs in supernatural miracles is given up. Earth can be experienced as a sacred place, and indeed, much of its beauty can bring tears to the eyes and great gratitude to one's soul; this "god," this sense of the sacred, this experience of "spiritual topographies," can be totally reconciled with modern science. But for the secular disbeliever, something else needs to be found to balance the outer and inner self.

What I am doing here is preparing for "our" first glimpse of the Grand Canyon, when we must be ready for the impersonal psyche in us to take the lead in viewing this great hole in the ground. The Grand Canyon can be conceived as a sort of archetypal typology. Its "Form" must be grasped. If we cannot do that then it is simply a big hole, an erosion specimen, a lesson in geography. One must leave one's modern ego stashed in the trunk of the car, along with one's camera, iPad, iPhone, "humility", and many other toys. You must bring only eyes and brush the dust off your soul.

One's eyes must be thirsting for the non-normal, for something more than even a pretty view. One must anticipate something that is known throughout the world, and indeed, is considered by most to be *the* grandest physical place on earth. Thoreau wrote a good deal about the power of anticipation, and such anticipation is needed when one approaches the rim. Keep an open mind, anticipate an experience, but let it dictate to you what it is all about. And if you are a teenager, please don't utter "awesome," a word that has been worn out and means far less than it is supposed to mean, which is "the sacred." Follow your emotions and see if "awesome" comes on its own, not by habit. Take your time, and do not think you have to take a picture of the "Hole." Let the experience do to your soul what it is capable of; there will always be time later to take shots of the canyon or pick them up on the Internet or the many stores. You will forget the pictures; you will not forget the possible soulful impressions that can last a lifetime.

And what do we mean by soul? I feel "soul," for example, every time I pick up one of my tools, as old and worn and sometimes dull as one could imagine. Clearly, these objects have no soul, and yet, to hold a tool with which I have worked for years, is to experience a feeling of friendship. Like my tools, the Grand Canyon has no soul, but there can be a *relationship* between canyon and human soul. To find it you must allow the canyon to speak to you, it must be waited upon; impressions take time and sustained attention. One look from a crowded point is not enough, not for *this* canyon.

When one looks straight down into the abyss from the rim, only in some places can one see the Colorado River (a mile down), or the Tonto Platform (3,000ft below the rim) laid out like frosting on a cake, separating the river from the cliffs, the strangest of sights. The eye glimpses the dazzling natural pyrotechnics on display up the wall of rock, level upon level, as it rises to the North Rim from the Inner Gorge—an enormous variety of reds, oranges, pinks, light and dark, depending on sun and shadow. From the South Rim (at 6,700–7,100ft, lower than the towering cliffs of the North Rim, 7,900–8,300ft) one can gaze down the canyon, either east or west, for 50 miles and have an immediate sensation of sheer immensity.

From the popular lookout at Mather Point, all this is taken in quickly with an overall impression of complexity within comprehensive, sweeping grandeur, but the eye moves quickly down to the Tonto Plateau, perhaps because it is right below and you can see the faint line of trails going in and out, around the side canyons of the Colorado, but in a world of their own, far above the Inner Gorge's river. So much of the canyon is inaccessible to the average hiker, but the Tonto Plateau (or Platform) does beckon. It seems to be something of a human paradise of plain, flat, grey-green land stretching east and west beyond sight, nestled between the frightening depths and heights on both sides. The very flatness of the Tonto Plateau— situated between the sheer drop of the South Rim and the North Wall's distant cliffs, terraces, peaks, and plateaus—is unexpected.

The second wave of excitement should be the immensity of it all. Quickly it becomes obvious that the "Grand Canyon" is really a collection of canyons, of hundreds, perhaps thousands, of side canyons, and all appear immense. The collecting "agent" is the Colorado River, visible here and there through the edges of the Inner Gorge, about 2,000ft below Tonto Plateau.

Next, comes the sensation of complexity; everywhere is the regularity of sedentary layers, but they are all too often broken by erosive features of different dimensions. As one looks up, there is the mishmash of buttes, towers, plateaus, temples; look down and there are the amphitheaters, gigantic basins created by enormous runoffs over the millennia.

Then the beauty strikes one—not pastoral soothing beauty, but a disturbing beauty. It is as if beauty and fear are interacting with one another. Some have called it "the sublime." It speaks to the human soul.

After the initial visual impressions, one hears the silence. It seems to rise up from the abyss, as if silence had a moving body, it's a *heavy silence*. It reminds me of the writings of the Swiss philosopher Max Picard (1888–1965), who personified silence:

> Where silence is, man is observed by silence. Silence looks at man more than man looks at silence. Man does not put silence to the test; silence puts man to the test. One cannot imagine a world in which there is nothing but language and speech, but one can imagine a world where this is nothing but silence. Silence contains everything within itself. It is not waiting for anything; it is always wholly present in itself and it completely fills out the space in which it appears.

—*The World of Silence*, Max Picard (Regenery Press, 1948).

Every time I come back to the Grand Canyon and peer over the rim, I feel that the place is greeting me with its silence. One should not be embarrassed by the anthropomorphic treatment of nature; it was common until very recently and even today we sometimes speak of "Mother Nature."

If one finds places on the rim—and there are many—where one can be alone while looking down and across the abyss, the silence becomes a curious mystery, for you realize that you have never, or very seldom, experienced such a thing in your life. You must live far into the country to experience true silence, and even then, it is possible to surround yourself with modern noises that push it away. In rural flatland or even on mountainsides there is movement and sound all around, but here the immensity of the canyon relegates any such activity to insignificance—one hears nothing below. And the silence is magnified if one stares over the rim at night, for then the eyes are useless while the ears are everything, and the "audible" silence is amplified.

Immensity, followed by complexity, followed by sublimity, and then silence—this is what they mean by calling the place "grand."

If you continue looking, since you do not *have to take pictures*, your eye comes back to that Tonto Plateau, it intrigues and beckons. It looks rolling rather than towering, a sharp contrast to all else around it, and its grey-green-brown subtlety of color seems almost domestic. The plateau seems to sway this way and that, flowing around the side canyons, its layer distinctly separate from all that is below and above it.

The topography of the Grand Canyon is the result of water acting upon stone. Each of the hundreds of side canyons are funnels for water that drops into the amphitheaters—bowl-like headwaters filled with canyon debris. For years on end, these side canyons can remain dry, but then, in a moment, the heavens open and water rushes down the courses of the canyons, scouring out sand and gravel and even boulders, dumping all into the Colorado River below. This is the intellectual, scientific understanding of what happens in the Grand Canyon. But those side canyons, those watercourses, are more than just pieces of earth—yes, the rushing water carries solid debris, but it also carries the canyon's psyche.

The ancient Greeks allowed Tyche, the Goddess of Chance or Fortune or Luck, to play a close role in *Moira*, one's personal destiny or fate. We moderns, on the other hand, try to remove luck from our lives, replacing it with control and planning. But, when solo backpacking in the Grand Canyon, it is essential just to let things be, planning only to the extent necessary to survive and to satisfy the "Backcountry" officials. There is no Wi-Fi (yet, to my knowledge) and no cell phone reception until recently on the rims. Instead, there are only the sounds and sights of nature.

There are some tools that one should carry in: a modern camping stove, some lightweight utensils, a plastic hand shovel to dig a hole for your waste, a lightweight tent (to avoid the packrats and mice, which can wake you up constantly through the night if sleeping without a tent), a mat and sleeping bag, a small LED flashlight, matches, some food, and a few clothes (days are hot, nights are cold). I also carry two collapsible hiking sticks, and a few medical items. Take a map of the trails, but no compass—use the sun and the time of day. Even packing only the bare essentials, your backpack will ultimately weigh between 50lb and 70lb, perhaps more.

Once, when coming up the Kaibab trail, with my pack considerably lighter than it had been since I had consumed almost all my food and water during my week below, I met a day hiker coming down. As he passed me struggling upwards, he exclaimed in a bellowing voice, "You animal!" He was right and I smiled at him, a smile of deep contentment. I did feel like a pack mule. It is good for the soul to be alone for a while, a concentrated week or more, and to rely on very little beyond one's own body and wits. Then, when you meet someone who appreciates your effort, it is a joy to hear them praise you. It is not that you have "conquered," it is, rather, that you came with an open, anticipating mind, and the canyon did the rest.

There is a common notion of the "value of nature"—its only value is that it offers the possibility of scientific breakthroughs. The only contribution of publicly funded scientific projects is that they eliminate superstitions—subjective feelings and religious belief in miracles—so that the public will support more and more scientific projects (going to Mars, exploring distant galaxies, researching black holes, etc.). In the process, no one seems to have asked if there is a downside to such a one-sided pro-science and technology culture. Could it be the "loss of soul"?

This dichotomy was first introduced to the Western world in the 1850s by the Parisian intellectual, Auguste Comte (1798–1857), who called his thought "positivism." Positivism is the belief (Comte even called it a "religion") that science is the *only* way to obtain truth, real objective truth. With such a perspective, still common in American universities, there can be no subjective truth, no psychic truth, just superstitions or undesirable opinions. If you come to the Grand Canyon with that outlook, you will not understand this book, and more importantly, you will obtain no psychic transformation by hiking the Grand Canyon. Positivism creates a large blankness, a psychic vacuum, into which all manner of tragic evils will rush.

In his book, *On the Rim* (University of Minnesota Press, 2001), Mark Neumann tells of a woman who, upon seeing the Canyon for the first time, complained of "feeling like a fly." Neumann concludes from this that "if a young girl was disturbed before the canyon's fearsome quiet (she had called it 'so horribly, horribly quiet'), perhaps it was because she sensed an obligation to feel as special as those who filled the pages of magazines with their personal testimonies to silence."

Later in the same book, Neumann reflects on how many tourists associate the Grand Canyon with the movie of the same name, or with *Thelma and Louise*, or *The Brady Bunch*, or *National Lampoon's Vacation*. He seems to be saying that the large American middle class tries to keep up with the cultural obsession for environmental *gnosis* (false knowledge) by identifying with movie or TV characters, for it is the only way they can rise above their lives and find a surrogate elitism of their own.

As well as taking six solo backpacking trips along the Tonto Trail and the Tonto Plateau, I have visited the canyon rims perhaps a dozen times and have repeatedly heard first-time viewers say, "It looks unreal." Most do not expect the massive panorama of extraordinary topography strung out in front of them, but unlike their now familiar *virtual reality*, this is truly real. And yet... The Grand Canyon is so different from other canyons all over the world, that it evokes a strong sense of uniqueness and genuine "awesomeness." It evokes an undeniable sense of "un-reality."

Here is the enigma: here is not just a plateau cut by drainage, but an immense volume of earth that has disappeared, trillions of cubic feet of material that have been washed away by erosion over immeasurable time. This makes one think the Grand Canyon is a mystery. It is 12 to 15 miles across the abyss, from rim to rim, and the hole is so deep that it produces three seasons at once: winter at the rim, spring on the Tonto Plateau, summer at the bottom beside the Colorado River. The canyon is huge, deep, and from east to west, seems to go on and on (the Grand Canyon National Park is some 250 river miles long). One must wonder why the earth gave way just in this spot and what force could have removed so much earth?

When first confronted with the enormity of the Grand Canyon, evangelicals think of the Biblical flood. I am not such a literalist, but I do sympathize with the reach for a mythological explanation. However, the real explanation is found in geological evidence and scientific speculation, which, I insist, does not conflict with the mythological because geology and mythology are quite different kinds of expression and thought, and function in quite different ways within us. I use the abyss of the Grand Canyon as a metaphor for the abyss between these two incommensurables: inner human experience on the one hand, and scientific description on the other. They are parallel worlds, both equally important, and they intersect only in the human *psyche*, where they become a "coincident of opposites."

One of the major dimensions of the Grand Canyon is its history, both geological and human.

The people of this country will never get back to their roots until the vast majority of us consider nature to be the main show, nature not as cheap entertainment, but nature as "food for the soul." America's roots are in the pre-technological world of walking and "packing in." Before the railroad came, it took days to reach the Grand Canyon, no matter where one started.

> Nearly everybody, on taking a first look at the Grand Canyon, comes right out and admits its wonders are absolutely indescribable—and then proceeds to write anywhere from two thousand to fifty thousand words, giving full details.
>
> —Journalist Irvin S. Cobb, quoted in Scott Thybony,
> *The Incredible Grand Canyon: Cliffhangers and Curiosities*
> (Grand Canyon Association, 2007)

First, before we delve into examples of words that try to explain the uniqueness of the Grand Canyon, let's review a little of the history of the Park and the South Rim.

Theodore Roosevelt visited the Grand Canyon in 1903 and uttered the famous words about it, so often quoted and never followed: "Leave it as it is. You cannot improve on it, not a bit. The ages have been at work on it, and man can only mar it."

The Grand Canyon had been given protection as a Forest Reserve in 1893. In 1906, Roosevelt declared it a national monument, making use of the Antiquities Act passed that same year. In the ensuing years, many Parks were established by acts of Congress, while the Grand Canyon, widely seen as the greatest scenic place in America, was ignored! It was not until 1919—three years after the establishment of the National Park Service and a full twenty-six years after the Forest Reserve status was initially granted—that the Grand Canyon National Park was established.

To this day, many Americans mistakenly believe that the Grand Canyon must have been established as the first Park, but it was beaten by:

Yellowstone 1872
Sequoia and Yosemite 1890
Mt. Rainier 1899
Crater Lake 1903
Wind Cave 1903
Mesa Verde 1906
Glacier 1910
Rocky Mt. and Hawaii Volcanoes 1915
Haleakala and Lassen 1916
Denali 1917

It was not until 1975 that Marble Canyon was incorporated into the Park.

Part of the reason for the delay in granting the Grand Canyon National Park status was tied up in mining rights. Some of the finest deposits of uranium anywhere in the world are to be found in and around the Canyon—discovered by early miners looking for gold and copper. The U.S. government simply did not know how to accommodate the mining claims or, indeed, the Native Americans who claimed the "Indian Garden" area as their own home.

In 1903, Emery Kolb (1881–1976) took the now-famous photograph of Teddy Roosevelt leading a mule party down the Bright Angel Trail, followed by John Hance, the colorful early canyon pioneer and first non-native resident of the Grand Canyon, after whom the Hance trail was named. For me, this photograph references the legacy of ambivalence always present at the Grand Canyon: we do not want men to improve or mar the canyon, but each of us wants easy access, wants to be rescued if we get into danger, wants interpreters of geography and geology, *and* wants a modicum of aloneness within it, requiring, of course, a batch of regulations and the building of a modern "village" with its consequential parking and noise problems. We do *not* want to pay much in terms of effort and sacrifice to experience nature in a meaningful way. In other words, we are much conflicted, and rather childlike in the worst connotations of that word.

When the National Park idea was in its youth, and before the national highway system was built, getting to any of the Parks was arduous. At the Grand Canyon, the railroad came to serve the El Tovar Lodge, which opened its doors in 1905. Down the hill from El Tovar, the site now occupied by Bright Angel Lodge (built in 1935) was nothing more than a small wood-frame hotel, a cabin, and a series of tents. Indeed, in the pioneer mining days before the establishment of the Park, only those who lived on the rim or *had* to see the canyon took the journey.

When the Grand Canyon became a National Park in 1919, what is now called Center Road offered the first access to the rim through the Village. Until that time, limited development had been spread out along the rim, from Hermit to Grandview, with no exclusive emphasis on the Village. Then, in the 1920s and '30s, the Entrance Road headed up to Mather Point and looped around to the southwest before heading to the Village. This created parking problems along the road to Mather Point, which were resolved by the building of the Canyon Visitor Information Plaza.

The centrality of the Village was instituted by the Park Service when Stephen Mather, the first National Park Service Director, incorporated two policies: the creation of the Corridor "Sacrifice" policy (i.e., the centralization of all tourist services) and the establishment of a single concessionaire who would want the financial benefits of high-density, money-making activities in one place accessed by the railroad. The first concessionaire, the Fred Harvey Company, with its "Harvey Girls," was associated with the railroad, as was Mary Colter, the architect of the Grand Canyon.

The Park Service's job was, and is, to "serve the public," and yet the public has always wanted a broader, less concentrated spread of services at the Grand Canyon. Regardless, the management imposed their concessionaire's desire upon the public, producing a concentrated Village where all the accommodations—including the *one* campground—are located, whether the public likes it or not. This action was justified by the Corridor "Sacrifice" policy.

2. Reflections on Historic "First View"

The Grand Canyon: Early Impressions, edited by Paul Schullery (Pruett Publishing Co., 1989) is a compilation of recorded first impressions of the Grand Canyon. It opens with the words of General John Wesley Powell (1834–1902). His text is an understatement of the dangerous and historic nature of his 1869 trip—his expedition was, after all, the first time a white man had journeyed down the length of the "Marble and Grand Canyons." After admitting that he and his party did not know what lay before them, Powell wrote: "Ay, well! We may conjecture many things. The men talk as cheerfully as ever; jests are bandied about freely this morning; but to me the cheer is somber and the jests are ghastly." He then proceeds to describe the nature of the river and the cliffs in detail. Some of his men would later panic and try to climb out of the gorge, only to be killed by Native Americans.

> We are three-quarters of a mile in the depths of the earth, and the great river shrinks into insignificance, as it dashes its angry waves against the walls and cliffs that rise to the world above; they are but puny ripples, and we but pigmies, running up and down the sands, or lost among the boulders. The river is insignificant in size compared with the entire canyon, and the men even more so, but merely in size.

In Powell's writing, there is none of the modern observation that the Grand Canyon makes a human *feel insignificant* in relation to it and the time spent in evolution's forming of it. It does not occur that the sense of being "pigmies" may therapeutically slow down the lust for exploration and then, following in its wake, the development of the "wild West."

I find it interesting that Powell could not understand why the Native Americans lived at the foot of what he named "Bright Angel Creek." The ruins of their dwellings are still visible today, on the Kaibab trail between the Black Suspension Bridge and the Bright Angel Campground. On one of my trips to the Grand Canyon, I spent several hours sitting on the side of the ruins, getting a feel for what the ancient inhabitants must have felt about life in that place. Powell speculated that since the natives must have been primarily an agricultural people, and there was little cultivatable land in the canyon, they must have chosen "a third alternative, and rather than be baptized or hanged, they chose to be imprisoned within these canyon walls."

However, the Spaniards did not come this far north and west to seek out the conversion or killing of natives; rather, they were too busy seeking the "Seven Cities of Gold." Powell's assumption is that the Native American shared his sensibilities and focused primarily on survival and succeeding in one's chosen line of work; no surprise that he calls the Grand Canyon "so barren a region." It would never have occurred to Powell that perhaps the Native Americans derived a benefit from the beauty of the place or that the Anasazi placed high value on dramatic geography.

Charles Dudley Warner (1829–1900), a popular essayist and contributing editor to *Harper's Magazine*, is the first noted author to write of the Grand Canyon, in 1891. The Grand Canyon Natural History Association records that the first tourist reached the Canyon in 1884, so Warner is writing just seven years later. He proclaims that Shelley's "Prometheus Unbound" does not match that of the "sublimities" of the Grand Canyon—hardly an endorsement except for intellectuals. He combines "the sublime and the beautiful," and yet there is no part of the subjective, in the modern sense, in his description of what he called "the Kaibab [Plateau] division," which has ever since been considered the "heart of the canyon."

Warner describes his first view thus:

> We took a few steps, and the whole magnificence broke upon us. No one could be prepared for it. The scene is one to strike dumb with awe, or to unstring the nerves; one might stand in silent astonishment, another would burst into tears. There are some experiences that cannot be repeated—one's first view of Rome, one's first view of Jerusalem. But these emotions are produced by association, by the sudden standing face to face with the scenes most wrought into our whole life and education by tradition and religion. This was without association, as it was without parallel. It was a shock, so novel that the mind, dazed, quite failed to comprehend it.
>
> —Charles Dudley Warner (Harper's Magazine, 1891)

Warner goes on to use the common terms "vastness," "transcendent beauty," and "transcendent suffusion of splendor." What the Grand Canyon is transcending, he does not reveal. If the term is religious—and at that time "transcendent" meant inexorably "having to do with God" or "created by God"—then the unparalleled nature of the Grand Canyon, with regard to Rome or Jerusalem, breaks down. Apparently, Warner is saying that he has not seen anything quite like the Grand Canyon before. It seems to me that religion is an inner matter and should not be projected onto a natural park—to do so does justice to neither religion nor park. Warner cannot do without projecting his citified and cultural biases into the Grand Canyon: "And here, indeed, is the idea of the pagoda architecture, of the terrace architecture [...] it is a city, but a city of the imagination." The last thing to which I would compare the Grand Canyon is a city!

Despite the reference to "pagoda architecture," it was not Warner but Clarence Dutton, an American geologist (1841–1912), who named many of the peaks that carry eastern religious names, such as Brahma and Shiva Temples, the Tower of Ra, Cheops Pyramid, and Zoroaster Temple. According to Julius Stone (1907–1985), writing in *Canyon Country*, there was a "long standing debate over exotic names in favor of indigenous ones," and Stone believes that it is "pleasingly appropriate" that the peaks that are "distant, unattainable and shrouded in mystery" carry such exotic names.

Of course, many Christians have been slighted by the use of only eastern religious names in the Grand Canyon, but somehow, I feel it would be inappropriate to have a "Jesus Christ Peak" or a "St. Paul Butte."

By 1926, the plague of locusts had arrived at the Grand Canyon thanks to Henry Ford's motor car, which now brought as many people to the South Rim as did the railroad. Of course, the railroad pulled in once a day, whereas the automobiles were destined to form a steady stream all day and even most of the night. Winfield Hogaboom, writing in 1902, tells the account of the first automobile to reach the South Rim using the line of the Santa Fe Railroad, traveling 65 miles from Flagstaff. Hogaboom, Oliver Lippincott of Los Angeles, and one T.N. Chapman, newspaperman, also from LA, arrived together at the rim. There, Hogaboom recounts, "I stood [...] upon the rim of that tremendous chasm and forgot who I was, and what I came there for."

Apparently, he was motivated by what I will call "firstism," the desire to be the first to visit with an automobile—firstism is a disease that still infects a particular clan of hikers and climbers. Hogaboom exclaims, "Before me lay the sublimest panorama in the world." Then, two days later, "Chauffeur Lippincott drove the thing (the automobile) to within six inches of the rim [at Grandview] with its own steam and held it there while I took its picture."

Thus began the reign of the three-headed monster at the Grand Canyon—**firstism, motorcar, camera.**

One of the most famous tourists to reach the Grand Canyon and to give his account of his experience was the famous conservationist and self-designated caretaker of the High Sierras, John Muir (1838–1914). Upon seeing the scope of the canyon, he said, "Fortunately, nature has a few big places beyond man's power to spoil—the ocean, the two icy ends of the globe, and the Grand Canyon." If only that were true. From our perspective in the first decade of the subsequent century, we can only laugh at Muir's proclamation that "the locomotives and trains are mere beetles and caterpillars, and the noise they make [at the Grand Canyon] is as little disturbing as the hooting of an owl in the lonely woods." Today, one can hear the train whistle from the Tonto Plateau, and the crowded Bright Angel Trail bears witness to the arrival of the motorcar traveler just as much as the hordes at the Bright Angel Lodge's plaza bear witness to the arrival of the tour bus.

Muir makes an interesting observation, however, after repeating Major Powell's measurement of the Grand Canyon to be "about two hundred and seventeen miles long, five to fifteen miles wide, and from about five thousand to six thousand feet deep" he says:

> So tremendous a chasm would be one of the world's greatest wonders even if, like ordinary canyons cut in sedimentary rocks, it were empty and its walls were simple. But instead of being plain, the walls are so deeply and elaborately carved into all sorts of recesses—alcoves, cirques, amphitheaters, and side canyons—that, were you to trace the

rim closely around on both sides, your journey would be nearly a thousand miles long.

—*Steep Trails*, John Muir (Houghton Mifflin Company, 1918)

Muir relates his first impression in the customary way: "I cannot tell the hundredth part of the wonders of its features," and then spends several lines trying to do so. After many attempts to describe the object, he turns to the subject, the observer, although he mixes his impressions with his tendency to mix nature with a tincture of religiosity:

It seems a gigantic statement for even nature to make, all in one mighty stone word, apprehended at once like a burst of light, celestial color its natural vesture, coming in glory to mind and heart as to a home prepared for it from the very beginning. Wildness so godful, cosmic, primeval, bestows a new sense of earth's beauty and size. Not even from high mountains does the world seem so wide, so like a star in glory of light on its way through the heavens.

—ibid.

This mountain man seems here to embrace the Grand Canyon as even more wonderful than "his" beloved Sierras, for in the very next paragraph he mentions both Yosemite and the White Mountains, which in his observation evoke in the tourist a "gushing and sputtering" aloud like waterfalls, whereas in the case of the Grand Canyon, "for a few moments at least, there is silence, and all are in dead earnest, as if awed and hushed by an earthquake." Muir also compares the Grand Canyon to Yellowstone, with the former's multitude of colors winning out, even though Yellowstone became a national park much earlier than the Grand Canyon. For sheer description, Muir's account is the best I have read, although most of him is left out, with just a trace of modern "reciprocity" or "self-referentialness" showing here or there. His is a semi-religious account, although his love of nature, like Thoreau's, was forcing him away from transcendent religion and toward a "sacrality" found between the human soul and the outward experience of nature:

The whole canyon is a mine of fossils, in which five thousand feet of horizontal strata are exposed in regular succession over more than a thousand square miles of wall-space, and on the adjacent plateau region there is another series of beds twice as thick, forming a grand geological library—a collection of stone books covering thousands of miles of shelving tier on tier conveniently arranged for the student. And with what wonderful scriptures are their pages filled—myriad forms of successive floras and faunas, lavishly illustrated with colored drawings, carrying us back into the life of a past infinitely remote. And as we go on and on, studying this old, old life in the light of the life beating warmly about us, we enrich and lengthen our own.

—ibid.

Here Muir uses his elaborate analogy to bridge between two objects, the Grand Canyon and a library. He slips into the analogy between the canyon and the human experience of it only in the last sentence, and then only in the cliché of "we enrich and lengthen our own." Not yet has the canyon enthusiast become as important in this relationship as the canyon itself.

The Western novelist, Zane Grey (1872–1939), wrote "An Appreciation of Grand Canyon" in 1922, and it is here that the subjectivity of "first views" begins to emerge. Grey's cowboy tales, along with the much later musical, *Paint Your Wagon*, were a popular outlet for what intellectuals now call "the Myth of the West" or "the Cowboy Myth"—powerful but out of date and, nowadays, to be deplored if still believed.

Grey, who used to hunt mountain lions in the Grand Canyon and on its rims, began his essay by quoting William Allen White's essay in *McClure's Magazine* of 1905:

Once more the strange, infinite silence enfolded the canyon. The far-off golden walls glistened in the sun; farther down, the purple clefts smoked. The many-hued peaks and mesas, aloof from each other, rose out of the depths. It was a grand *and gloomy* scene of ruin where every glistening descent of rock was but a page of the earth's history. [my italics]

71

The paradox of the canyon being simultaneously grand and gloomy introduces the theme of time, a major constituent of the Grand Canyon experience. The Cowboy Myth is all about individuality, man facing nature, perhaps for the last time. Grey starts his own two paragraph piece thus: "To see the Grand Canyon full of purple smoke at dawn or sublimely fired at sunset, is to be elevated in soul." Although contemporary depth psychologists, especially the Jungians, speak of soul, they are few and far between, and almost no depth psychology is taught in American universities. "Soul" has lost out to "mind," the latter having the connotation of that which is conscious and can be explored scientifically. But for Grey, the Grand Canyon experience was all about soul and he ends his short essay: "...to feel the silence and loneliness of the desert—all this is to grow young again. And to taste the air, water, and meat of the open is to go back hundreds of years, when man was savage and free."

Here is the sense of "free from modern civilization." Here "savage" carries a positive tone, not the negative tone of White's paragraph. Modern man has lost not only his soul but also the sense of being a savage, underlying the inflated ego.

Here, too, is one revelation of why the Grand Canyon not only fascinates, thrills, and exalts its viewers, but also frightens us, somehow, beyond the dangers inherent in hiking it. It is a vast ruin that produces a sense of gloom in the midst of all else that is positive and inspiring. I call this "the downward theme," a major but most often overlooked aspect of the subjective response to the Grand Canyon. "Up" is the direction of inspiration, as for our mountain peaks, whereas "Down" is the direction of depression, of scary depths, as found in caves or gorges. Our culture subscribes to the idea that good leads *up* to heaven, while bad leads *down* to hell. But this needs revision or, more precisely, reversal—good is to be found in the downward thrust into the "depths," while the upward thrust leads only to the expansion and inflation of ego, a pathology.

Zane Grey moves closer to the mystery, which he sees embedded in the Western cowboy theme, but which I believe was conceptualized by Henry David Thoreau when he uttered the anthem of environmentalism, "In wildness is the preservation of the world."

Here's Grey:

[The Canyon] brought to my mind a faint appreciation of what time really meant; it spoke of an age of former men; it showed me the lonesome crags of eagles, and the cliff lairs of lions; and it taught mutely, eloquently, a lesson of life—that men are still savages, still driven by a spirit to roam, to hunt, and to slay.

—*Tales of Lonely Trails,* Zane Grey (Hodder and Stoughton, 1922).

We see this theme of the connection between "wildness" and freedom emerge time and again. West has always been, until recently, a metaphor or symbol of an anti-civilized freedom and individuality. Thoreau, who never saw the great American West, spoke often of the meaning of the West, associating it with freedom. He was once asked why, with his great love of Nature, he did not go west to find gold and the wilderness he desired. Thoreau answered by pointing inward, toward subjectivity, saying it was "wildness" within, not literal wilderness, that he sought, and also that "the earth is auriferous [gold bearing] everywhere." For Thoreau gold became a metaphor for the secret meaning of life—alchemists called it "the philosopher's stone." Thoreau further declared he had been hunting for "a hound, a bay horse, and a turtle-dove" throughout his life, having lost them when young, apparently meaning that his quest of "savageness" meant the loss, literally, of ambition (the hound), honor or success (bay horse), and friendship or love (turtle dove). The conflict here is between two layers within a human being—the civilized and the "still" primitive, now understood by depth-psychologists as "the collective unconscious." Thoreau's ambition, success, and love came only with an early death and the posthumous fame as the writer of *Walden.*

In his turn, Grey is introducing us to what James Hillman calls "the animal soul"—an ideal sought by many contemporary

73

Americans who have given up on institutional religion and politics and are looking for something with which to replace them. However, the lust to roam, to hunt, and to slay now must turn on our cultural problems: we must slay gnostic self-righteousness after roaming the canyons of psychic nature, hunting the elusive psychic balance. I suspect that many more solo hikers have crossed over the line that separates the object from the subject, and in so doing have brought those two opposites into a union, as Colin Fletcher (1922–2007) did on Beaver Sand Bar, when his "oceanic feeling" transformed him from just a long-trail hiker to an explorer of the element of soul (see Colin Fletcher's *The Man From the Cave* [Vintage Books, 1982], and *The Secret Worlds of Colin Fletcher* [Knopf Doubleday Publishing Group, 1990]).

It is not that Grey ignores the other side of the canyon's subjectivity, its "silent teaching." After all, it was he who wrote "To see the Grand Canyon full of purple smoke at dawn or sublimely fired at sunset, is to be elevated in soul." Rather, he says, the inspired elevation and the casting down into the gloomy, terrible abyss, are to be found together, and must be seen in relation to one another.

An Englishman by the name of John Boynton Priestley (1894–1984) visited the canyon in 1935 and wrote an article for *Harper's*. Once again we hear the refrain: "There is of course no sense at all in trying to describe the Grand Canyon. Those who have not seen it will not believe any possible description. Those who have seen it know that it cannot be described." He goes on, of course, to try by comparing it to "a revelation" and to Beethoven's Ninth Symphony "in stone and magic light." This amusing suggestion, however, is worth contemplating: "Every member of the Federal Government ought to remind himself, with triumphant pride, that he is on the staff of the Grand Canyon." Aye, if only! And Priestley does understand the problem: "There must be in the soul of this great country a certain large noble simplicity that is hardly finding any verbal expression at all. The people who feel it cannot find the right words. The smart loquacious people [the professors] cannot feel it." Another of Priestley's well-deserved digs is aimed at the professors and their students: "I thought of the fascination that Paris seems to have for so many clever young Americans. Hanging there, wondering, on the brink of the Canyon, this fascination seemed the most preposterous thing and Paris itself a mere distant doll town."

No survey of first impressions of the Grand Canyon would be complete without mention of John Burroughs (1837–1921), who visited the Canyon in 1909 with John Muir, with whom he had previously traveled to Alaska. Burroughs was in his early seventies by this time and was a noted nature writer with a shy temperament. He noted the "indescribable" aspect, and almost succeeded in bypassing the temptation to try a description, saying only, "We speak of it as a scene: It is more like a vision, so foreign is it to all other terrestrial spectacles, and so surpassingly beautiful." He quoted Charles Dudley Warner: "I experienced for a moment an indescribable terror of nature, a confusion of mind, a fear to be alone in such a presence."

There are also those visitors who react with apparent nonchalance, something I have witnessed often among the tourists lounging around the area where the Bright Angel Lodge and steak house are situated. They will invariably be looking at their smart phones as if these technological gadgets are a defense against the canyon's siren call toward nothingness. A few years ago, a TV ad showed a large-screen TV placed on the rim of the canyon, displaying a picture of the canyon. A group of pre-teens was seen gazing at the screen rather than at the real thing just beyond! The message was that you don't have to drive to the Grand Canyon when you can see it from the comfort of your own home. Or, if you insist on driving out to it, you can experience the Grand Canyon at the Tusayan movie theatre, while avoiding the fee and the traffic at the National Park itself.

Warner wrote of a friend who...

...wished he could have been present with his Kodak when we first looked upon the Grand Canyon. Did he think he could have gotten a picture of our souls? His camera would have shown him only our silent, motionless forms. I wished at that moment that we might have been alone with the glorious spectacle, or that we might have hit upon an hour when the public had gone to dinner. The smoking and joking tourists sauntering along in apparent indifference, or sitting with their backs to the great geologic drama, annoyed me. I pity the person who can gaze upon the spectacle unmoved. [...] I could even sympathize with the remark of an old woman visitor who is reported to have said that she thought they had built the canyon too near the hotel.

Burroughs described his impression from Hopi Point, not his very first view of the canyon but perhaps the most interesting. He imagines a hiker emerging from the woods at Hopi Point:

You get glimpses of a blue or rose-purple gulf opening before you. The solid ground ceases suddenly, and an aerial perspective, vast and alluring, takes its place; another heaven, counter-sunk in the earth, transfixes you on the brink. "Great God!" I can fancy the first beholder of it saying, "what is this? Do I behold the *transfiguration of the earth*? Has the solid ground melted into thin air? Is there a firmament below as well as above? Has the earth's veil at last been torn aside, and the red heart of the globe been laid bare?" If this first witness was not at once overcome by the beauty of the earthly revelation before him, or terrified by its strangeness and power, he must have stood long, awed, spellbound, speechless with astonishment, and thrilled with delight. He may have seen vast and glorious prospects from mountain-tops, he may have looked down upon the earth and seen it unroll like a map before him; but he had never before looked *into* the earth as through a mighty window or open door, and beheld depths and gulfs of space, with their atmospheric veils and illusions and vast perspectives, such as he had seen from mountain summits, but with a wealth of color and a suggestion of architectural and monumental remains, and a strange almost unearthly beauty, such as no mountain-view could ever have afforded him" [first italics are mine, second are Burroughs'].

Burroughs also contrasts the perspective and personality of Muir to those of himself—Muir prefers mountains, Burroughs favors the depths of this great, mighty canyon. Inspiring heights are now juxtaposed with depressive depths, and since the former is the majority motif of American culture, the latter becomes the greatest challenge and major threat.

On the second day of their visit, the Muir party was led down the Bright Angel Trail; Burroughs was third in line with his great white beard and overcoat—they were riding through snow—and Muir was bringing up the rear, with his own great white beard but a suit, no overcoat, looking rather contemptuously upon the rest of the train, which included two women, as if to say, "You think this is cold. Try sleeping with a thin blanket on top of an 11,000ft Yosemite peak in the dead of a Sierra winter!" Alas, the interplay of ego and nature!

Burroughs wrote, "that veteran mountain-climber and glacier-meadow Scotsman John Muir pooh-poohed the scheme. 'Go up,' he said, 'and not down. Climb, climb; do not fancy that you can bestride a mule and go down into that hole and find the glory that lures you from the top.'"

Muir's religious asceticism and "God-is-up" mentality make one wonder why he partook of the ride at all. Burroughs responded to his friend:

> There is always satisfaction in going to the bottom of things. Then, we wanted to get on more intimate terms with the great abyss, to wrestle with it, if need be, and to feel its power, as well as to behold it. It is not best always to dwell upon the rim of things or to look down upon them from afar. The summits are good, but the valleys have their charm, also; even the valley of humiliation has its lessons.

Having apparently felt he had the better of Muir, Burroughs tells us that "the sarcastic Scotsman, seeing that we were not to be ridiculed out of the adventure, reluctantly consented to be one of the misguided parties." And he gives us a geological fact with a meta-phorical meaning: "Water and sand are ever symbols of instability and inconstancy, but let them work together, and they saw through mountains, and undermine the foundations of the hills."

I will suggest here that the metaphor of depth applies to the human psyche as evoked by the canyon. The more one stands look-ing down into the Grand Canyon from the rim, the more one thirsts for an intimate contact with what is below, an analogy for the desire to get to the bottom of life's mystery.

These early responses to the canyon are similar to contemporary responses—unaware that they are so doing, they project the soul's needs into the place. It is what one brings to the Grand Canyon that is primary.

Thoreau writes beautifully about this theme in *Walden*: "Let us settle ourselves, and work and wedge our feet downward through the mud and slush of opinion, and prejudice, and tradition, and delusion, and appearance, that alluvion which covers the globe." And elsewhere: "I wanted to live deep and suck out all the marrow of life, to live so sturdily and Spartan-like as to put to rout all that was not life..." Yes, indeed, that is exactly what the solo backpacker does—he must live a Spartan life because he must carry everything he needs upon his back.

3. The Shamanic Sipapu

What does shamanism and the Native American vision quest have to do with the Grand Canyon? One answer, the superficial one, is obvious: Native Americans believe that the Grand Canyon is a sacred place, and that one particular place, just up the Little Colo-rado before it flows into the main Colorado River, is believed to be "the center of the world," what they—primarily the Hopi peo-ple—mostly call "the sipapu." More than this, the Grand Canyon was home to the *Anasazi*—a Navajo word meaning the Ancient People—along with the Cohonina and the Cerbat. The Anasazi are believed to have taken up residence in the Grand Canyon from about 500 CE until about 1200 CE, when it is believed that a climate change began to force them out until, by 1300 CE, they had left for good. Today's Bright Angel Trail follows the course of an ancient footpath that led down to Indian Garden and was created by the ancient Havasupai, who were descended from the Cerbat. Finally, there is an Anasazi ruin just off the South Kaibab trail before one reaches the Phantom Ranch area, and there is a Shaman's Gallery, off the North Rim's Point Sublime. It is one of the best-preserved sites of prehistoric art anywhere in the world and comprises a sloping back wall some 7ft high and 60ft wide, it is believed to have been the ceremonial center for the ancient natives, the elder shamans. The site was described and photographed by Seymour Fishbein in his *Grand Canyon Country: Its Majesty and Its Lore* (National Geographic Society, W.D.D., 1991), but the route to, and location of, the gallery is kept secret by the Park for fear of vandalism. Today the Havasupai live in the area just west of the Great Thumb Mesa, in Havasu Canyon.

While a university professor, I taught "The Philosophy of Native American Religion" for some twenty years and take the subject seriously, believing that we can learn much from it. In the course I differentiate between a philosophical and a historical approach to Native American Religion; the latter approach is common while the former, I have never encountered. It was a difficult course to teach, for students expected me simply to adhere to the politically correct approach that Native Americans were victims of white supremacy and to explore nothing else. I called this "the Dancing with Wolves" approach, a morality play in which all natives are good, all incomers are bad, and all nuances are damned. After we discussed and explored the veracity of this treatment, we would discuss the "trail of tears," the slaughters, relocations, and manipulation of Native Americans—the history. Understandably, modern Americans want to grieve over the treatment of the Native American in the past. They do not, however, apparently want to learn from them today.

The philosophical approach to Native American religion identifies with shamanism, about which my students typically knew nothing, and which I spent most of the course teaching to them. Rather than telling them simply that Native Americans were victims of white, racist Americans, which is *obvious*, I told them *why* that was so—modern Americans are not taught that they, too, have evolved from shamanistic history, and thus, in the historical sense, are no different from Native Americans.

I think that modern white Americans can learn from shamanistic Native Americans, and that the reverse is also true. To do that requires an absence of scapegoating, a desire to live in the present, and a distancing from our gnostic morality perspective, where we show our superiority by denigrating "the other." It requires an understanding of what it means "to be living close to nature," and the ability to think philosophically about the difference between cultures, rather than just embracing them all equally, without critical reflection on their differences. It is the politically correct cultural relativism that gets in the way of my courses, for I do not have a psychic need to feel personally superior. My psyche wants the truth, the whole truth, and nothing but the truth, not a "truth" consecrated "by God" or by institutions, or by the scapegoating of others. In his book, *Shamanism: Archaic Techniques of Ecstasy* (Pantheon Books, 1964), Mircea Eliade makes the necessary distinctions:

> ...though the shaman is, among other things, a magician, not every magician can properly be termed a shaman. The same distinction must be applied in regard to shamanic healing; every medicine man is a healer, but the shaman employs a method that is his and his alone. As for the shamanic techniques of ecstasy, they do not exhaust all the varieties of ecstatic experience documented in the history of religions and religious ethnology. Hence any ecstatic cannot be considered a shaman; the shaman specializes in a trance during which his soul *is believed to leave his body and ascend to the sky or descend to the underworld*. [my italics]

Eliade was an old-fashioned scholar who wanted to be seen as a historian, and never sought to interpret shamanism in its mystical/ mythic nature. Of course, the shaman did not fly to the sky or to the underworld, not literally. Rather, the description of the shaman's soul "leaving his body" is a description of the experience of ecstasy, of leaving one's ego-body (the body known by the ego) and to find an altogether different and much more wonderful self, one that could be called "soul" or "psyche." Also, the shamanic "trance" is nothing less, or more, than a concentrated period of imagining and thinking, it is not something "pathological." Simply put, genuine shamanic experience is part of the inner journey: it begins in childhood, progresses through adulthood when myths, spiritualities, and classical philosophical learning, the love of wisdom are part of one's personal curriculum, and finally evolves into old age when ecstasies result in the meeting of one's conscious and unconscious in a middle ground, *metaxy*, that of balance.

Hence, my psyche tells my brain to ask: "Are Native American religions closer to nature than those of white culture?" I ask the question because the answer is not, for me, easy. Taken literally, they are not closer to nature; an absence of any scientific understanding of the world does not relate to a close experience of nature as ecstatic joy. We must realize that both "soul/psyche" and "collective unconscious" are imaginative constructs, not "things" that can be found in the human body or brain or heart. In *The Soul of Shamanism: Western Fantasies, Imaginal Realities,* Daniel C. Noel focuses on *Healing Fiction* by James Hillman. He quotes Hillman: "...both daimon and unconscious are modes of imaging, modes of writing fictions, and both have their healing efficacy as the case may be."

Noel then continues:

> Hillman certainly learned from Jung, a scientific psychoanalyst who nevertheless built a bridge *from* the concept of the unconscious over *to* the imaginal power of the psyche. Hillman extends the bridge even further in the direction of the arts, by means of the arts, in this case re-visioning

the scientific as well as the unscientific terminology as different ways of imagining, but more specifically as different modes of 'writing fictions.'

—Daniel C. Noel, *The Soul of Shamanism: Western Fantasies, Imaginal Realities* (Continuum, 1997)

This, then, is the question: Is the Native American closer to nature than today's environmentalists? There are those who assume the answer to be 100% in the affirmative. If, however, the truth is even slightly less than 100%, then Native Americans can learn something from some of us. But, if that is the case, and I think it is, that does not mean that we modern Americans cannot learn a great deal from Native Americans. I believe a relationship of reciprocity is preferable to a one-sided one that caters, or condescends, to the other side.

I did not start my hikes into the Grand Canyon with much thought about the local Native American history, but I ended by understanding that two of my trips were a form of "vision quest," somewhat like those of the shamans. And the sipapu, the great hole that connects the underworld (our unconscious) with this world of conscious development, became for me a centering around my deep-nature absorptions in the Grand Canyon, in Monument Canyon, and in Cremation Canyon.

The best single thing we can learn from shamanism is that there is a real sense in which nature, and most particularly the beauty of nature, is sacred. The one thing that I would wish to offer Native Americans or contemporary shamanism is that it should be demythologized. Shamans, for example, do not fly literally but, rather, are specialists in *senex* wisdom: they are what Jung called the archetype of the "wise old man."

Here is an example: Black Elk was a shaman of the Oglala Sioux, and in 1932 a book was written about him as told through John Neihardt (Flaming Rainbow). The book, *Black Elk Speaks: Being the Life Story of a Holy Man of the Oglala Sioux*, was reprinted in 1959, 1961, and 1972 (Bison Books). In its third chapter, called

"The Great Vision," we read that, when Black Elk was nine years old, he heard voices. On one occasion, he was eating with Man Hip, a man who liked him, in his tepee when:

> While I was eating, a voice came and said: "It is time; now they are calling you." The voice was so loud and clear that I believed it, and I thought I would just go where it wanted me to go. So I got right up and started. As I came out of the tepee, both my thighs began to hurt me, and suddenly it was like waking from a dream, and there wasn't any voice.

This was the start of the youthful shaman's experience. The next morning, he said, while riding with other boys, "my legs crumpled under me and I could not walk." The day after, he experienced his arms and legs being "swollen badly," as well as his face.

Here was the start of what made Black Elk a "shaman," a wise man in his tribe. His sickness, indicated by the hallucination detailed above, was strange, having come upon him so suddenly. But then the vision "healed" him, and he was put in the line of his Grandfathers, among whom, undoubtedly, a previous shaman had existed. The tribe knew that Black Elk had heard voices and, when he told his parents he was "called," they were predisposed to welcome this vision as a literal happening.

This was just the start of "The Great Vision," which featured a great man, horses of different colors, "a skyful of horses dancing round me," and the boy was promised "a council with your grandfathers." At one point the boy heard "the winds at war like wild beasts," making him prophesize: "I am afraid something very bad is going to happen all over the world." The narrator stresses that: "He [Black Elk] cannot read and knows nothing of world affairs," ostensibly so that the reader will believe that Black Elk, indeed, has the magical power to see into the future and had not heard of the impending World War I.

The important point gleaned from Black Elk's story is that to be recognized as a shaman, two essentials must be present: there must be a childhood calling of some sort that leads to hallucination, and the shaman-to-be must have the courage, psychologically or literally, to leave his family and tribe and turn away from the ordinariness of everyday life—a considerable loss, regardless of the circumstances.

This "breaking loose" of the collective unconscious ("dissociation") should not be considered a mental breakdown, as an ordinary psychiatrist thinks, but rather as an attempt for the young boy to learn about himself without either interpreting evil or ignoring the experience as mere idiosyncrasy. I do believe that Black Elk was partly psychopathic, as suggested by his vivid hallucinatory experience, but I also understand why his tribe accepted him as a shaman. Tribes of that time could not differentiate between extraordinary illness and shamanic wisdom because both, in their own way, are extraordinary. Black Elk gave the tribe an unusual experience, and as they listened to him describe that experience, they understood the unusual as sacred or transcendent. It was the tribe's psychic need for a sacred leader, like the ancient grandfathers, that made them believe in Black Elk's unique powers. His power was not that of flight, but rather, his sense of calling from the elders; it might be called a "constructive hallucination." His uniqueness was hidden in his "illness," the swelling that was psychosomatic and the "calling" that was part of the shaman's inner journey.

There is one last crucial consideration of shamanism. In Eliade's massive book on the subject, there are two passages that I will put together:

> The symbolism of the "Center" is not necessarily a cosmological idea. In the beginning, "Center" or site of a possible break-through plane, was applied to any sacred space, that is, any space that had been the scene of hierophany and so manifested realities (or forces, figures, etc.) that were not of our world, that came from elsewhere and primarily from the sky.

> The shamans did not create the cosmology, the mythology, and the theology of their respective tribes; they only interiorized it, "experienced" it, and used it as the itinerary for their ecstatic journeys.

The first segment comes from Eliade, the historian of religion, who sticks to the historian's model of scholarship—giving the facts without theorizing about them. That is why Eliade says that the shaman's "hierophany" (the manifestation of the sacred) leads to what the shaman takes as real forces, figures, etc., that come from another world or "primarily from the sky." The second segment tells us what Eliade knows, but he reveals very little, for fear that he will not be considered a dependable historian. Eliade knows that "sky" is a symbol for "another world," and that "other world" is itself a symbol for the collective unconscious revealed by the shaman and repressed by the shaman's tribe. It is "collective," but also unacknowledged except by the shaman. The "ecstatic journeys" of the shaman are the only genuine interpretation of shamanism. They cannot be artificially induced, but a charismatic leader can easily manipulate a group into believing that they are experiencing an ecstasy. There is an incommensurability between that of group dynamics—about which Freud wrote an entire book—and that of the genuine deep-nature-absorption experience and especially the ecstasy that it sometimes brings. While Eliade, to my knowledge, never used the word, "demythologization," it can nevertheless be applied here—the shaman uses the group's theology or cosmology of mythology as "the itinerary for the ecstatic journeys."

Two backpackers in a streambed with a "pointy-topped" peak on the distant horizon. *Photo by Gary Ladd*

CHAPTER 3

THE ART OF TURNING AROUND

Side Canyons
. . . .

1. My First Solo Trip

2. The First Stop

3. The Sublime

4. The Failings of Nature Worship

On the New England coast, nature is somewhat mild. To a Westerner, the mountains of Massachusetts, New Hampshire, and even Maine are little more than "foothills." Even Mt. Washington, a 6,000-footer with some of the worst weather in the world, is nothing of much note. Through my forties, living and working in the Boston area, I was too busy to recognize my need for dramatic nature, but, by the time I was approaching fifty, things had begun to change. As winter moved into March and the university closed for spring break, I came up with the idea of writing a book about the Grand Canyon and asked the university for a sabbatical. By the time they agreed, it was summer.

I got hold of a copy of John Annerino's *Hiking the Grand Canyon* (Sierra Club Books, 1993) and looked at his recorded average temperatures at different times of the year. In March, the South Rim averages 51 degrees Fahrenheit maximum, 25 degrees minimum—at the top of the two main trails, snow and ice would not be melting much through the night. Annerino also gave temperatures for the Inner Gorge—in March, the maximum temperature there was 71 degrees, the minimum 48 degrees. In June and July, the Inner Gorge could see temperatures above 100 degrees during the day and somewhere in the 70s at night. But at 4,000ft, Horseshoe Mesa should be much cooler than the Inner Gorge, and so I decided that from the end of June through the beginning of July would be an excellent time to hike the Grandview Trail to Horseshoe Mesa. I borrowed a backpack from a friend and bought the appropriate trail food, almost all freeze-dried. I had an old camp stove and sleeping bag, and an old tent. I was ready to go.

I had no idea how uninformed I was, but I was about to find out.

1. My First Solo Trip

Hiking the canyons of the southwest was not my wife's idea of a vacation, so she suggested I go alone. My father agreed to transport me from my parent's home in Idyllwild, California to the Grand Canyon, where he would camp in the South Rim campground. While I sorted out flights from Boston, I also sourced a few more reference materials. I had decided that I would take pictures—something I had never done before while hiking—and would make notes of my experience, so a decent camera and some paper and a pencil were added to my pack. I purchased *The Heart of the Grand Canyon* map (1978), as recommended by Annerino. On closer examination, however, I realized that while Horseshoe Mesa was partially on the map, the Grandview trailhead was not. Annerino also recommended the "Geological Map of the Grand Canyon National Park, Arizona," a very large map that he suggested should be cut up, but not knowing if I would ever return to hike in the area, I ignored his advice. Instead, I decided that when I arrived at the Grand Canyon, I would buy the National Park map.

I read through Annerino's equipment list for overnight hiking and bought only what I considered to be absolutely necessary. I ignored the "gaiters and instep crampons, the waterproof tent, space blanket, ground cloth, poncho and rainsuit"—after all, I was going in the summer, and besides, my borrowed backpack was rather small, and I didn't have room for all that stuff.

After a short visit with my parents, Dad drove me across the desert and into the Park. He had decided to sleep at the park in his Dodge Van, while I slept in my tent. I went to the store to buy a map, and by the light of my camp lantern, I perused the Grandview Trail. It looked like an easy, short descent. Indeed, the guidebooks listed it as the fourth easiest trail, but one without a lot of traffic. I was more convinced than ever that I had picked the right trail and would have no problem. The trail was only 3 miles long, and I was going to stay on the Mesa two nights, so I would have plenty of time to find water at Grapevine Creek down on the Tonto Plateau, if I needed it.

When we arrived at the campground, the temperature was in the high 80s, and by the time I had gone to the Backpacker Reservation Office, got my permit, and returned to make dinner, it had climbed into the 90s. I made a mental note to carry plenty of water when I set out.

Once more I opened Annerino's book. I knew that the trail dropped 2,474ft from the top to the Mesa, and I also knew that the Mesa was only 932ft above the Tonto Trail, so it might not be as cool as I would like. Then, I came across Annerino's description of the trans-canyon trails, such as Grandview Trail down to the Mesa. My eye crossed his data for the "Seasons"—"take the Grandview in Fall through Spring," he wrote, "Summer can be deadly."

WHAT? I read the words again. "Deadly," "Summer…"

I paused, but then thought, this was *early* summer. I was going 3 miles, I would take lots of water, I would be all right.

The sun was setting and the temperature at the rim, 4,000ft above the Mesa, was still in the 90s. I spread my tent on the ground, without erecting it, and laid my sleeping bag on top—I was not afraid of wild animals in the one and only campground on the South Rim, filled with people. It was too hot to sleep in a tent, and my old-fashioned tent was not well vented.

In the morning, having slept well, I had a quick breakfast with Dad, and then we set off. It was still early, the sun just beginning to hit the roads.

Dad dropped me at the Grandview trailhead and we said our goodbyes. As I began my descent, some things were bothering me: I was carrying a borrowed pack, with an external frame that was not at all comfortable. I had not practiced walking with it, indeed, had made no specific preparation for this trip, relying instead on my overall good health and fitness. But there was that newly developed bulging spinal disk, caused by a weekend of overdoing it while landscaping at a house I had recently built. And there was the heat. Just before Dad had dropped me off, we heard on the van's radio that the temperature in Phoenix that day was likely to break the city's record high. Even at the Grandview Trailhead (7,400ft), it was very warm, and it wasn't even 9:00 a.m. yet. But, I reasoned, I was barely going down into the Canyon, so it shouldn't be too hot, it was still only 3 miles, I was used to vigorous exercise, and I was still relatively young.

From childhood recollections, I knew that the Grand Canyon was a marvelous place; what I didn't appreciate was that it not a "nice place"—not in summer, below the rim.

From the outset, I experienced small twinges in my back—no doubt aggravated by swinging the pack into and out of the van—but they were not bad, and I was now committed. Dad would not be back until the third day, and anyway, I had a burning thirst to go down into the canyon. Plus, now that I was on my way, I was quite excited.

The trail was a constructed trail, built by miner Pete Berry, superimposed on an old Hopi trail, in order to work the Last Chance Mine in 1890. The mine was a dud, and Berry quit searching for his fortune. He turned, instead, to building the Grandview Hotel and guiding the increasing number of tourists down to the Mesa. But, while it was man-made, according to Scott Thybony's *Official Guide to Hiking the Grand Canyon* (Grand Canyon Association, 1994), the Grandview Trail is a designated wilderness trail, which means it is not maintained and has some difficult sections—Annerino hadn't mentioned that!

But Grandview Point is quite accessible by car and not far from the Corridor (Kaibab to Bright Angel), so surely, I reasoned, the National Park authorities would not have let the trail deteriorate entirely. I had seen the top of the two *maintained* trails—the Bright

Angel Trail and South Kaibab Trail—and they were both covered with mule and horse excrement; that couldn't be good. Since mules did not go down the Grandview Trail, I thought my choice was a good one. It did not occur to me that the reason only the two corridor trails are maintained is *because they are mule trails.* Nevertheless, as I reached the first switchback, I consoled myself—such a beautiful trail must be well-maintained, even if not quite to the standards of Bright Angel.

I soon arrived at one of the "difficult spots" of my wilderness trail. After a few switchbacks, the trail straightened out and went beneath an overhanging ledge. My pack's top scraped the underside of the rock even if I walked on the very outside limit of the trail. I bent down, and immediately a spasm shot through my spine. I fell to my knees, took off my backpack, swung it around to my front and, holding it to my chest so that I could just barely see over it, struggled to my feet, and walked the 15ft or so under the overhang. By the time I made it to the far end, I was sweating profusely. But I had done it and, after some trail mix and water, decided—with absolutely no supporting evidence—that "it must be easy from now on."

As I swung my backpack around to replace it on my back, a grommet came loose and one of the shoulder pads became detached from a ring on the bottom of the pack—now the pack wasn't just uncomfortable; it was also broken. Not for the last time I wished I had invested in a new internal-frame pack. My mood sank. I was suddenly aware of the engulfing heat, surely well over the 120 degrees forecast for Phoenix, and here I was on a sun-soaked trail, with a broken pack, an almost-broken back, no other human anywhere near, and it was still early morning.

I looked through my pack for something with which to jury-rig the pack. With a piece of string and my Swiss Army knife (thank God I had not done everything wrong), I rigged up a temporary fastener, put the pack on a rock, slid into it so as not to stress the weak repair, and continued my descent, wondering what else could go wrong.

Toward the bottom of the slope, just before the trail turned north and shot for the ridge, the temperature must have been close to 150 degrees. By then, I was somewhere between the Coconino Sandstone and the Hermit Shale, less than halfway to my destination, in terms of elevation, and only about a quarter of the way in terms of trail-feet. As I made my way down the sometimes-loose rock and the sometimes-2ft or more down-steps, my back was giving me shooting pains every fourth step or so.

2. The First Stop

I had to stop. I decided to remove the pack, calm my back, drink lots more water, have my lunch, and do some serious thinking about my situation. One of my favorite philosophers, Jose Ortega y Gasset (1883–1955), used to say: *"Yo soy yo y mi circunstancia"* (I am myself and my circumstance). It was time "myself" took a good hard look at my circumstance.

There is something about eating that helps with thinking. It became clear to me that, in spite of the "only 3 miles," I was not going to reach my goal without risking heat exhaustion or, given that the highest heat of the day was still before me, possibly a life-threatening heatstroke. I had brought what I considered to be a lot of water, but if my back really played up, then I would likely not have enough. I knew it could take a day or two to calm down my back, so I couldn't afford to go down to the Cottonwood campground for water. And who knew how long this unbearable heat was going to last? If only I could find some shade; looking down the trail there was none to be seen.

Perhaps it had been the presence of my father and not wanting to give up without even trying, but I now realized that what I was doing was insane. All at once, I felt totally unprepared and totally foolish.

I had, at last, reached the point of true fear. I had read about deaths in the Grand Canyon and had no desire to become one of the statistics. I was alone, I had no one to blame but myself, and no one but myself to pressure me into continuing. Risking death for a contrived target that meant nothing to anyone but myself was neither sensible nor defensible. It was time to turn around and go back.

My ordeal was far from over. I had 800ft of climbing ahead of me and the spasms in my back were excruciating. I would take it as easy as possible, drink and rest as much as possible, and take all day to get out if necessary. I also knew that, if it became necessary, I would simply abandon my pack.

And yet, despite everything, despite my rational self, something in me still clung to the dream of carrying on. Could I? After I rested for a while? Couldn't I?

I was sitting on a rock at the edge of the trail and, for the first time, noticed a prickly pear blossom, fully open and of a bright pinkish color. It brought me a moment of calm and I spoke to it: "Thanks, you beautiful flower, thanks for being right here. You are the high point of this morning walk." I opened my lunch sack and, focusing exclusively on the flower, I drank and ate. And then, in a moment of life-saving lucidity, I decided to convince myself that the discovery of that flower had been the purpose of my trip. As foolish as I had been, the notion of beauty and purpose calmed me.

After taking in a tremendous amount of water and finishing my sandwich, I got to my feet and headed upward. Little step after little step, I was going back. My pack was now a little lighter, since I had drunk much of my water, and I dragged and swung it up the trail until I was past the dreaded overhang. It took me close to an hour.

Then, I carefully picked up the pack and held it close to my chest. For the rest of the excruciating climb, I would carry the pack in front of me, and keep my back as straight as possible. I stopped at every rock that was high and large enough for me to sit down without bending. As hour followed hour and step followed step, I forced myself to repeatedly drink and rest.

I reached the trailhead at about 4 p.m. Except for the encounter with the flower, it had been seven hours of misery. Just before the top, I met a young boy coming down; he took one look at me and scrambled back from where he'd come. He was the only person I saw on the trail that day.

At the trailhead, I inched myself atop a stone wall and stretched out, perfectly flat. It was far from comfortable, but it meant I could stay prone and motionless until someone found me. Within thirty minutes a tourist came by. I asked him to contact the Park authorities and have them find my father at the campground.

At last, my father arrived. I inched into the van's passenger seat, and we drove back to his campsite. The next morning, after a long night's sleep in the van, I was able to walk again, albeit only gingerly.

As Dad and I drove back to Idyllwild, I reflected on my failure— an honest facing of what must be done in order not to fail again or give up on backpacking altogether. Four things were obvious: One, if I did return to hike in the Grand Canyon, it would not be in the summer; Two, I would have to train hard before even thinking about trying again; Three, I needed to invest in new, appropriate equipment and pack wisely; Four, if I wanted to backpack in nature and survive, I must learn to observe and respect her signs.

3. The Sublime

> Where there is the tree of knowledge, there is always Paradise: so say the most ancient and the most modern of serpents.
>
> —Friedrich Nietzsche, *Genealogy of Morals*
> (Vintage: Re-Issue Edition, 1989).

One can go to the Grand Canyon with rational knowledge of the difficulties, the topography, the weather problems, the things one reads in books. But I have found it hard to be always rational about the place. The Grand Canyon is fascinating, and therefore one wants to go on hiking even when one is in trouble. I am not one to quit at the first arrival of pain. However, one must learn from pain, especially if one wants to achieve a high level of joy *despite pain and fatigue.* Balance is everything. Too little or too much physical effort should be eliminated if one is to enjoy oneself and avoid a trekker ego. There is no scoreboard in the Grand Canyon.

I had had many prior life-threatening experiences, but I swallowed my pride that day on the Grandview Trail. It takes only one unmanageable event to end a life. So why do so many hikers go on when everything is telling them to turn back? Because the ego's desire to conquer is irrational.

What sticks in my mind from my ordeal on Grandview Trail, even now, decades later, is the image of a flower. I would like to say that I turned around because I am a rational person, perhaps more rational than most. But I don't remember carefully reasoning with myself and deciding that I should turn around. In fact, I wanted very badly to go on and wait out the pain on the Mesa's flat ground. There were any number of reasons for turning around: it was so damned hot, I was drenched in sweat, I was in fear of a spinal rupture that could kill me. Annerino was right: death awaits someone who goes down any un-patrolled and un-maintained trail in record summer heat. And yet I had continued. Had continued until a chance encounter with a flower. Somehow, it was that flower that made me see sense and turn back.

Here I think of my mentor, James Hillman, who continuously emphasized the "image" as a key to opening the unconscious. Perhaps the possibility of near death evoked the unconscious, but it was the flower that opened it. Its beauty made me feel like a fool.

It occurs to me now that there was a deeper reason that compelled me to turn around, and ironically, it was the same reason that had compelled me to continue—the desire to experience *beauty.* Or, perhaps, *beauty and the sublime.* When I saw that single bloom, I saw sublime beauty, and it was that which made me overcome my pride and blank out all the perceived rational arguments for continuing. If so, then somehow beauty "outranks" rationality. Consider Plato—the only epistemological philosopher I know very well, and in my opinion, the founder of philosophy. Plato ranks beauty right up there with truth!

It has been said: that "fools rush in where angels fear to tread" (Johnny Mercer, 1940). The lyric of this popular song from the swing and jazz age went thus: *Fools rush in where wise men never go/ But wise men never fall in love so how are they to know/ When we met, I felt my life begin/ So open up your heart and let this fool rush in.* The implication is that real knowledge, that which can change your life for the better, comes from experience, not from facts.

In my experience, something "inner" saved me that day, and now I know that it was what the ancient Greeks called "the daemon," the inner voice. I had such illuminations on several occasions in my solo hikes, but I admit, it is hard to differentiate between what actually happened, and what I "recall." It wasn't as simple as believing that a magenta blossom made me turn back and thus saved my life. However, perhaps the flower evoked a state of mind agreeable to my daemon, whose job it is to get my mind to pay attention to my unconscious. The daemon is not "a guardian angel," for an "angel" is simply an outward projection of what is happening inwardly.

As I try to explain what I felt that day on the Grandview Trail, I recognize the immense gap between what I feel and intuit about my hikes, and the struggle I have in putting those experiences into words. I believe that philosophy runs into this problem more than any other discipline. James Rhodes (1916–1976), one of my favorite interpreters of Plato, addressed this very problem:

> For there is no writing of mine about these things [mystical philosophy] nor will there ever be. For it is in no way a spoken thing like other lessons, but, as a result of repeated being with and living with the matter itself, it is brought to birth in the soul suddenly, as light that is given off by a leaping flame, and it maintains itself thereafter.

> —James Rhodes, *Eros, Wisdom, and Silence:*
> *Plato's Erotic Dialogues* (University of Missouri Press, 2003)

Rhodes also writes of the dilemma of true philosophy:

> Philosophy is a constant proximity to its matter that has rewarded Plato with flashes of illumination that resemble lightning. The reality thus brought to light is called "nature." *Amathia* [ultimate spiritual ignorance] is overcome only when one has experienced such enlightenment. Plato cannot give the competent verbal instruction because words differ essentially from the flashes of illumination. By implication, Plato can only counsel the intelligent on how to position themselves in order to receive the flashes, or lead them in the same exercises that were the occasions of his illuminations. The inference tallies with Socrates' statement that education consists not in putting vision into blind eyes, but, rather, in "the turning around of the soul, so that it might see for itself." If Plato tried to set the wordless flashes to words, the many who do not live in abiding nearness to the matter, and who therefore are unlikely to receive the illuminations, would find no referents for the words. This would inspire unjust contempt in some and make others ecstatic about speech that, to them, was unintelligible.

—ibid.

The Greek word for the "turning around of the soul" is *periagoge* and is found in Plato's *Republic*. My turning around of the soul would happen in Monument Canyon, but my turning around on the Grandview Trail was external, and I think the two, the periagoge and the physical turning around, are interrelated. Specifically, I was not hiking to conquer some trail or gain some bragging right. I may have had a little of that in me at the beginning, but my Grandview disaster eliminated it.

At first, I did not want to discuss my Grandview Trail trip with anyone—it amounted to one day… it had been a failure. But that short-lived experience taught me something fundamental about the Grand Canyon: Yes, it is a place of sublime beauty, but it evokes fear as well as joy, and without the appropriate level of fear, one is dicing with death.

4. The Failings of Nature Worship

I know of various sources within the environmental movement who speak fondly of Everett Ruess (1914–c.1934) and can make the connection between this legendary young man and James Hillman's brilliant chapter in *The Soul's Code* (Random House, 1996) called "Growing Down." Hillman believes that once the individual has experienced the call or pull of the daemon, it is their task to bring this mythological, otherworldly force down into life lived in the body and in nature. Hillman quotes from Plato's *Republic* (X, 620e)—known as the Myth of Er—where, prior to birth, a soul must choose its life as well as the guardian of that life. Hillman calls it "the Platonic myth of growing down," for "the soul descends in four modes—via the body, the parents, place, and circumstances." The body must face "the sag of gravity"; the parents present the aging child with a family tree that the daemon insists should have meaning. Place, Hillman suggests, relates to "living in a place that suits your soul and that ties you down with duties and customs." For Hillman that place was a small town in Connecticut; for me it is Rockport, Massachusetts. And the fourth mode, he wrote, was found in "giving back what circumstances gave you by means of gestures that declare your full attachment to this world."

Thoreau also refers to the idea of "growing down." Here is a critical passage of his:

> Let us spend one day as deliberately as Nature, and not be thrown off the track by every nutshell and mosquito's wing that falls on the rails. [...] Let us settle ourselves, and work and wedge our feet downward through the mud and slush of opinion, and prejudice, and tradition, and delusion, and appearance, that alluvion which covers the globe, through Paris and London, through New York and Boston and Concord, through church and state, through poetry and philosophy and religion, till we come to a hard bottom and rocks in place, which we can call *reality*, and say, This is, and no mistake; and then begin, having a *point d'appui*, below freshet and frost and fire, a place where you might found a wall or a state, or set a lamp-post safely, or perhaps

a gauge, not a Nilometer, but a Realometer, that future ages might know how deep a freshet of shams and appearances had gathered from time to time.

—Henry David Thoreau, *Walden* (Princeton University Press, 1971)

The daemon, or genius, is a *puer* (young) figure or image, associated with the heights, with success, glory, and honor. However, our culture overestimates the heights, the climbing for success and fame, the need to conquer. The conquering trekker in the Grand Canyon, says James Hillman, knows little about "the darkenings and despairing that the soul requires to deepen into life." True optimism requires one to face the unknown and the tough aspects of learning, especially after a midlife crisis. The last phase in life is a going down of the body, the loss of some bodily strength, but it is also the culmination of the psyche, the reaching of joyful wisdom and coming into full contentment of oneself, with a continuous feeling of gratitude for one's life. Old age, therefore, requires that we overlook the falls and embrace "the fall" into the unconscious.

I have already suggested the corrective effect that a descent into the Grand Canyon can have on one caught up in this *puer* desire to rise and fly over things. But Hillman conversely claims that the effect of the daemon on one's life produces inexorable feelings of loneliness and exile (homelessness). These feelings can be broken down into four elements: "nostalgia, sadness, silence, and a yearning imagination for 'something else' not here, not now." All these elements can be found in what we know of the life of Everett Ruess and those who have built him up into a legendary figure.

We start with W.L. Rusho's (1928–) *Everett Ruess: A Vagabond for Beauty* (Peregrine Press, 1983). Ruess, a young man from Los Angeles, walked into the canyon wilderness (apparently the Escalante River canyons) and was never seen or heard from again. However, instead of identifying Ruess as a confused adolescent, for nature worshipers he became a heroic figure of legend, which I consider a mistake.

The life of Ruess is valorized and glorified by many in the environmental movement because they, and he, failed to "grow down," failed to bring the daemon into the lower level of life with its limitations and difficulties. Hillman suggests some of the ordinary ways in which this can be achieved:

> The heart's image requires efforts of attachment to every sort of anchoring circumstance, whether these anchors be the loyalty of friends, the stability of contracts, the reliability of health, the schedules of the clock, the facts of geography. [...] The heights seek the depths; one way or another they want to come down, even if by suicide, by ruinous contracts and bankruptcy, by entangling emotional messes.

> —James Hillman, *The Soul's Code*
> (Random House, 1996)

This explains why an elderly person will insist on a schedule and a continuous way of doing things, as if they were some sort of ritual: Up at 6 a.m., make tea, toast a bagel, read the morning newspaper, etc., through most of the day. Such "rituals" are an "anchoring circumstance," to use Hillman's language, something the young refuse to entertain, dismissing it with the youthful saying: "been there, done that."

Whether one is young or not, backpacking requires a consistency of "chores," with regard to tent, sleeping bag, cooking, water pumping, packing up, reading the map, applying suntan lotion, etc. In the case of the young or midlife person, heights can be opposed by the depths—tragic death, for example, or harm or addiction—whereas the mid-life transformation is a realization of the stability and balance of the psyche and allows for a youthful old age with a soulful and spiritual talent. Depths are no longer a danger or a threat, but a welcoming "anchoring," as in the process of centering, the *sipapu*.

Rusho's telling of the story of Everett Ruess carried an Afterword, written by Edward Abbey in the form of a sonnet:

> You knew the crazy lust to probe the heart
> of that which has no heart that we could know,
> toward the source, deep in the core, the maze,
> the secret center where there are no bounds.
> Hunter, brother, companion of our days:
> that blessing which you hunted, hunted too,
> What you were seeking, this is what found you.

What was it that "found" Ruess, and was identical to that which he was seeking?

Abbey, the legendary spokesman for the wild, monkeywrenching nature-advocate, seems to identify with young Ruess, and the "blessing" referenced in the sonnet apparently was an identity or merging with nature itself. Did that make Ruess commit suicide, which is my guess about what happened to him? Suicide is not always "intentional"; often the suicidal impulse strikes one when in "over one's head" and the danger kills—a direct consequence of the impulse, whether labeled "suicide" or "accident."

I think it likely that Ruess gave into the pull that the abyss or the precipice applies to the solitary "vagabond" in Canyon Country. Ruess talked indirectly about suicide and the romantic notion of "leaving no trace." Vanishing without a trace inevitably produces a legendary status in the one who vanishes, especially if such a person left rather vague, poetic, and quasi-philosophical letters behind. Even today there are many young who project their misgivings about society and their longing to "escape," not by drugs but by a lust for nature. I admitted to my lust for nature on the Grandview Trail, but I also know that I experienced my inner, "lower" or "deeper," nature on that same hike as I sat on the trail, faced my failure, and was rewarded with the flower. The old saying has its wisdom: try and fail, and then try and try again.

Everett Ruess has, for some time, been thought of as a legendary figure, and since conclusive evidence of what happened to him is not available, it is the figure that is of significance to me, both in its relation to what we know of the boy and what we know, or can come to learn, about ourselves. In an article in *The Navaho Times,* Rusho was asked about Ruess's legendary status, and answered, "I think it's because Everett's desire to escape civilization and experience raw nature is still very powerful today, especially among the young."

The paper reported further:

> In his 1942 book, *Mormon Country,* Pulitzer Prize-winning writer Wallace Stegner [1909–1993] described a search by Neil Johnson, a California placer miner, and John Terrell, a reporter for the *Salt Lake Tribune.* Johnson had read of Ruess's disappearance, and early in 1935 went to his parents' home in Los Angeles and knocked on the door offering to help. But it was hard to get an Indian guide to sign on with the party. At a desert trading post, when Johnson and Terrell announced that the fellow they were hunting might be dead, the Indians scattered.... UA Professor N. Scott Momaday, also a Pulitzer Prize winner, believes the myth that has grown up around Ruess compares with that of Billy the Kid. "Everett Ruess, like Billy the Kid, perpetuates the myth of the dying cowboy," Momaday wrote in *American West* magazine in 1987, about "that lonely heroic figure who bravely confronts his destiny because he must." Stegner described Ruess as an artistic athlete, a callow romantic, an atavistic wanderer of the wastelands. "But one who died—if he died—with the dream intact.
>
> "We might be inclined to laugh at the extravagance of his beauty-worship," Stegner continued, "if there were not something almost magnificent in his single-minded dedication. [...] If we laugh at Everett Ruess we shall have to laugh at John Muir, because there was little difference between them except age.

With Stegner, Momaday (1934–), and Abbey stimulating the legend, Rusho had to have made some money on his book. However, Stegner's judgmental portrait of Ruess—as "callow romantic and atavistic wanderer of the wastelands"—constitutes fighting words and something of a "minority opinion."

Like most, except perhaps Stegner, Rusho doesn't seem to know what it was that haunted Ruess. Rusho's book, published by Peregrine Smith Books in 1983, is little more than a source book of Ruess's extant letters. It features an introduction by John Nichols (1959–), author of *The Magic Journey, The Sterile Cuckoo,* and *The Milagro Beanfield War.* Nichols speaks of Ruess's "emergence with the landscape" as if it were totally positive and manifestly unproblematic. He uses Ruess's own characterization of himself as having "a reckless self-confidence," which Nichols tells us "enabled him to face the wilderness with an utter disregard for his personal safety." Here again are the words of a *puer aeternus,* which may be why Stegner called him "atavistic," for there is a lust for the primitive within such consciousness, an imagination that lifts its possessor above the physical and into an angelic, "numinous" dimension—part and parcel of archaic shamanism.

Here is Ruess praising himself:

> I have seemed to be at one with the world. I have rejoiced to set out, to be going somewhere, and I have felt a still sublimity, looking into the coals of my campfires, and seeing far beyond them. I have been very happy in my work, and I have exulted in my play. I have really lived.

However, a vision quest (if that is what Russ had embarked upon) is not very visionary if it ends in death. To be considered authoritative, the ancient shaman has to put himself into a trance, or be ill, or dream and take all that happened to him to be true. Thus, the shaman played the role of the wise old man for a society that took everything literally and "by the heart." This, surely, demonstrates that nature worship is too emotional and lacking in consideration and understanding.

The Greek myth of Icarus is a warning about the desire for the heights—it often results in a crashing down and dying. Grand Canyon obsessives know about canyon depths—in a slot canyon, the walls on each side often rise 1,000ft or more—but are illiterate about inner depths, those which are in all of us, recognized or not. It may be that most of those that backpack in the canyons are unconsciously seeking their inner depths with no proper awareness that they even exist. Indeed, when it comes to psychic depths, the younger you are, the less you know of the inner journey. This, of course, doesn't mean that a close relationship with nature is futile. But the worship of outer nature is often an indication of a lack of connection to inner nature and its journey.

Nichols quotes, apparently admiringly, these words of Ruess: "I have known too much of the depths of life already, and I would prefer anything to an anticlimax." Such youthful presumption does not stop him from saying: "Life on this earth is very precious and very beautiful. We must learn to heed the pure and delicate voices of those who cherish it." And yet, if we follow this to its logical conclusion, those who cherish life would not take the chances that Ruess did. No, what Ruess represented was an incipient secular gnosticism, what the Greeks called *amathia*, the ultimate spiritual ignorance—"I have known too much of the depths of life already." A young man is surely delusional if he thinks he has positively experienced the depths. Only through experience do we learn that depths are equal to heights, each designed by the nature of the psyche to balance the other. The Greeks called such balance or between-ness *metaxy*; the Navaho used the term *h'ozh'o*.

On my excursions into the Grand Canyon, I have been repeatedly drawn to the idea that the Tonto Plateau—roughly midway between the Inner Gorge and the South Rim—was a "spiritual topography" analogous to that of psychic *metaxy*. The ancient Gnostics bent Christianity into a literalistic and dogmatic cult, so that our modern secular world is now full of those who "know-it-all," even if they never took the time to learn anything in depth. The modern Gnostics, such as Ruess, consider communal life on this planet to be a prison in which their spirits are constrained, thereby creating a despair and desire to escape. Early Gnostics were antinomian, swinging between sadism and masochism. Either way, Ruess could not "grow down," to human life's difficulties; his death came on too high and too soon.

The daemon does not necessarily work things out for the best; all depends on whether the individual can listen to the inward call rather than bending to an outward preoccupation with what others will think of them. The young Ruess was a product of his parents—his father was a Unitarian minister out of Harvard Divinity School who was a fond reader of Emerson, and his mother was a follower of Isadora Duncan, the founder of the modern countercultural movement. Unable to assimilate and differentiate from such heady influences, Ruess died before his twenty-first birthday, a young man filled with conflicting tendencies, not yet mature, and surely not yet someone who should be looked to for guidance or inspiration.

I am reminded of a moment when the Transcendental Club (a group of New England intellectuals of the early to mid-1800s) was discussing Ralph Waldo Emerson's (1803–1882) recent European travels, specifically his exploration of the epicurean delights of Paris. Emerson turned to Thoreau and asked, somewhat condescendingly, "What dish is your favorite, Henry?" Thoreau replied simply, "The nearest." Thus was the difference between French post-modern sensibilities, and those of an American who knew he was "in his proper place" (see *The Earth has Soul: The Nature Writings of C.G. Jung*, North Atlantic Books, Berkeley, California).

Beauty can be treated in the same way as Ruess treated nature and Emerson treated travel: as something to elevate one's spiritual worth in the eyes of self and others. Ruess glowingly elevated beauty without cognizance of the sublime, the danger that could have spoken to his daemon had he had more maturity.

Nature lovers must learn also to love the nature of the "journey within," rather than dichotomizing themselves from the enemy, those who do not proclaim "lust for nature." Heraclitus was right: the psyche knows no limits—or at least none that we can reach—but that should not be our goal. Our goal should be the balance between ego and unconscious. Common sense will tell you that after a week or more in the wilderness, it is nice to go home to comfort; and after too long in such a comfy home, it is nice to get back to nature. I call it panological balancing. But there is no balance if nature equates with spirit. Spirit wants it all, as if it need not consider the reality of the earth. I learned from Hillman to always differentiate spirit from soul—the latter is more important and far more subtle.

Our culture is filled with the discrepancy between where one is and what one should be doing there. Consider Chris McCandless (1968–1992), who killed himself in an old school bus in Alaska; or Timothy Treadwell (1957–2003), who lived with bears that eventually ate both him and his girlfriend. The main reason why the wild outside does not offer sufficient salvation for the alienated modern consciousness is because the experience of beauty, when concentrated—as in the Grand Canyon—leads from pleasure to pain because it is *sublimely* beautiful, *beyond* beautiful.

> In the final analysis, we count for something only because of the essential we embody, and if we do not embody that, life is wasted.
>
> —Carl Jung, quoted by James Hillman in
> *The Soul's Code: In search of Character and Calling*
> (Warner Books, 1996).

Looking downslope, off-trail into a side canyon of Marble Canyon with one backpacker descending through the brushy, rubble-covered slope. *Photo by Gary Ladd*

CHAPTER 4

THE CORRIDOR TRAVAIL

Side Canyons

1. The Grand Canyon's Best Trail

2. Into the Depths

3. The Yucca Cache and a Ranger's Compassion

4. Indian Garden: Creek Cracks and Mulish Water

5. Horn Creek: Taking Note

March 13, 1992. I am fifty-one and setting out on my second attempt at a solo backpacking trip in the Grand Canyon. Following my disastrous outing on the Grandview Trail, I have thoroughly prepared for this expedition. I have all the equipment as suggested by numerous guidebooks and am hiking at the best time of year—it will be early spring on the South Rim, late spring on the Tonto Plateau, early summer down at the bottom of the Inner Gorge.

I have a new internal-frame backpack, a gas stove and two fuel bottles, three flashlights, a 4lb, two-person tent, lightweight sleeping bag, good hiking boots—two pairs—and a pair of Tevas for the campground. The cost has mounted, but I consider it an investment: I will have all this gear for the rest of my life, and many companies will replace or repair any damage, even if that damage is the result of normal wear and tear.

I have trained extensively, walking around the neighborhood carrying the backpack, as well as working out on the treadmill and exercising using various leg-strengthening machines at the gym. I'm ready to go.

I am staying at the Bright Angel Lodge the first night, in the backpacker's "shed." I have always loved the Lodge. It was designed by Mary Colter in a combined Native American and "modern naturalistic" style. There is a real-wood fireplace flanked by benches where backpackers can drop their packs, relax, and talk trips and tips with one another. Plus, the cafeteria serves reasonably priced meals in a sit-down-and-be-served style—might as well stuff one's belly to capacity before starting out!

I plan to descend to the Bright Angel Campground for my first night on the trail, following the South Kaibab Trail, rather than the more popular Bright Angel Trail. Then I will stay on the South Kaibab Trail up the Inner Gorge to Cremation for the second night, then over to Grapevine, along the Tonto East and away from the Corridor. After two nights in Grapevine, I plan to come back, retracing my route, through Cremation and out on the South Kaibab Trail. I have not purchased a water purifier, as I will stock up on water from the Bright Angel Campground. Then I will carry that water back up to Cremation to cache for retrieval on my return journey. At Grapevine, there is always water in the large canyon creek, so I shall also refill there.

In my room at the Lodge, I pack and repack my belongings. Beyond all the new kit I also have my clothing, coffee pot, spoon, cup, and some food staples in plastic bags. I'm not sure how much food and other gadgets I need, but I am following the guidebooks, so I have a snake-bite kit, matches in several water-tight containers, notebook, map, flashlights, candles, signaling mirror, whistle, thermal blanket, bandages, back brace, and another pot. When I swing the pack up onto my back, I estimate it weighs about 75lb, but I'm not worried. It feels good.

I figure I can use up all the water I carry on my descent to the Bright Angel Campground, because once there I can refill my canteens at the faucet. The water comes from the Roaring Springs up north in the Bright Angel Canyon and is piped down, across the Silver Bridge and then up to the South Rim, with another water fountain connection at Indian Garden. By getting an early start and caching a lot of my weight at the Tip Off (as the Kaibab is called just before it enters the Inner Gorge), I'll be able to walk my filled canteens back up to the Tip Off and then go the short distance into the Cremation section to camp my second night.

And so, to bed.

The next morning, early, I drive out to Kaibab Point (which you can no longer do), find a parking space, hoist up my pack, and begin my descent. The pack is heavy, very heavy, but my exhilaration at descending over the rim is overwhelming, and everything else pales into insignificance.

The canyon fills my senses with sights and smells, and immediately I rediscover the heavy, unique silence.

1. The Grand Canyon's Best Trail

In my opinion, the South Kaibab Trail is the best walking trail anywhere in the Grand Canyon. It is a ridge trail, one of only a few in the park. It follows Cedar Ridge out to O'Neil Butte and then continues to Skeleton Point, 5,217ft elevation; from the trailhead this is a drop of approximately 2,000ft. Beyond Skeleton Point, the trail descends quickly in a series of cobblestoned switchbacks, before reaching the long, moderate, straight slope onto the Tonto Plateau. From here you are treated to one of the best views of the Tonto Plateau, with Pipe Springs to the left and Cremation to the right.

From the trailhead one can easily reach Skeleton Point by noon, drink up, eat, rest, check the pack, and prepare for the 1,217ft drop to the Tonto Plateau. This red-wall descent is marked by steep, standard switchbacks, with no rock outcroppings or trees to offer relief from the morning sun. Immediately after dropping down from Skeleton Point, the trail consists of cobblestones set into the earth; their surface has been worn to dust by the mules that use this trail daily, and the trail is slippery, especially if one is carrying a top-heavy backpack.

From the Tip Off down to Phantom Ranch, it is red earth all the way, with long looping switchbacks. It presents little difficulty to the hiker, and even negotiating the tunnel and the black bridge over the Colorado is not hard. Indeed, the most important aspect of the South Kaibab Trail is not its expansive views but rather its lack of dangerous "exposures"—the technical term for a narrowing trail with no protection from the long drop along its edge. Exposures are common in the Grand Canyon, and many are simply terrifying.

That day, though, I had no such worries and was looking forward to an easy descent to Bright Angel Creek and Phantom Ranch. I would not be there in time for breakfast, but I could buy a box.

Such was my plan.

The South Kaibab Trailhead is next to Kaibab Point, and nowadays one must take the Green Bus from the Canyon Visitor Information Park. There are portable toilets ("handyman toilets") at the trailhead bus stop, but no water fountains. Except for the first quarter mile or less, the South Kaibab Trail is in the sun and thus does not suffer with spring ice. It begins, as all Grand Canyon trails do, with a series of switchbacks through the Kaibab limestone, but they are only a couple hundred feet in length. There are always, inevitably, other walkers at the beginning of the trail, but when hiking solo, one soon learns to ignore others and take care only of oneself. The trail is steep in its descent (only 7 miles down to the Bright Angel Creek)—which is why I chose it—but it meant that I had to take it slow and easy, taking care to control both myself and the extra weight of my full pack. I was relaxed—after all, I had most of the day for my descent.

In his book, *Hiking the Grand Canyon* (Sierra Club Books, 1993), John Annerino says that the South Kaibab Trail "was constructed by the National Park Service in 1924 primarily as an alternate to the Bright Angel Trail because hosteller Ralph Cameron had a franchise based on mining claims that allowed him to charge a $1 toll to anyone riding or hiking down it." Cameron's franchise lapsed in 1928, and so the park had two trails. In that same year, the park service built the suspension bridge, called "the black bridge," across the Colorado. Each one-ton cable was brought down the Kaibab by Havasupai men, who, it was said, would deposit their load and then *run* back up to the top.

Mules were first introduced to the Canyon in 1919 by miners and have been used for work and pleasure ever since. Scott Thybony's book, *The Incredible Grand Canyon: Cliffhangers and Curiosities from America's Greatest Canyon* (Grand Canyon Association, 2007), contains a picture of the Union Pacific workers topping out on the Kaibab, all riding mules, in heavy snows in 1937. At that same time, Marvin Gandy designed a mule-mounted litter, like a stretcher, on which an injured person could be stretched out along the mule's back with their head just behind the animal's neck and their feet at its rump. Ironically, Gandy became the first to use his invention when he was rescued from the canyon after suffering an appendicitis attack. In 1964, Apollo astronauts trained in the Grand Canyon by walking down the Kaibab, but even they chose to come back up by mule.

I made light work of the first part of the trail, hiking down to the restrooms at Cedar Ridge. Here, there were some rocks and logs to sit upon, and I spent a few moments looking at O'Neill Butte, before continuing on my way. As I walked, I found myself wondering: who was O'Neill?

According to Scott Thybony, "Bucky" O'Neill prospected in the Grand Canyon during the 1890s and helped to bring the railroad to the South Rim. But he was best known for raising a band of Spanish-American War fighters under the auspices of Teddy Roosevelt, called "the Rough Riders." He ended his days in a fierce gun battle with the Spanish. When he and his men came under heavy fire, Bucky refused to take cover, proudly proclaiming: "The Spanish haven't made the bullet that will get me." He was shot in the head and died instantly.

I continued to make good time from Cedar Ridge all the way to Skeleton Point, but the weight of my pack was bearing down on me as I struggled to control my descent along the eight or so switchbacks below the point and I had to slow down drastically. Unfortunately, I had not brought walking sticks and, along with the excessive weight that I was carrying, I now saw this as a mistake. It also occurred to me that an umbrella would have been useful for shade. So much for all my planning!

By the time I made it to the toilets, just after the South Kaibab Trail crosses the Tonto, I could not get the pack off quickly enough—the weight had become untenable. I decided to divide my load and cache part of it within a large yucca plant. The sharp yucca leaves would protect my possessions from animals and, perhaps, inquisitive humans!

Decision made, I drank most of my water and tried to rest my legs. I now considered an alternative to my itinerary: I was going down to the Tonto and could spend the night at Bright Angel Campground. Then, the next day, I could return and continue on to the east, into Cremation. I thought I had been smart by not carrying much water, relying instead on the guaranteed water at Grapevine. But, even without the water, my pack was too heavy, and I hadn't counted on the effect of the total load on my legs. I could feel them shaking and was sure there was some considerable pain coming my way soon. Clearly, I hadn't trained with sufficient weight at home. Apparently, I was still an amateur at Canyon hiking.

My legs were shaking a little as I stood, and I knew that I had to give them at least 15 minutes of rest. What I didn't know was that I was suffering from a buildup of lactose in my legs. I should have lain down and propped my legs up on my pack. If given enough time with one's legs higher than one's head, the lactic acid drains out of them. No one had told me this and I had never read of it in any of the guidebooks. Thus, after a rest that was both too short and wrongly positioned, I put my pack back on (now 30lb or 40lb lighter) and went over the Tip Off.

The trail followed long switchbacks and there were now no cobblestones and few rocks to negotiate. It was dusty but partially shaded and I settled into an easier descent. Nevertheless, despite all the improvements, my legs did not feel good; the shaking had stopped, but they were aching, and I knew I would have trouble even getting down to the campground, much less making it back up the next morning with the water. It began to occur to me that, once again, I had not planned things well. I should have taken far less stuff, more water, and should have stopped for the first night in Cremation. Furthermore, if I had packed a water filter, I could have found water either in Cremation or the Boulder Creek area, or I could have turned around and walked back up the South Kaibab Trail after a night's sleep. That would have meant only a 4-mile hike down from the rim—a reasonable walk with a backpack large enough for a week's stay.

All this I realized and mulled over as I made my miserable descent. It was all wishful (or rueful) thinking for, as things were, I had no choice but to continue. I had to make it to the water. If not, I would surely die. Already it felt like summer on the Tonto Plateau, and I knew that it would only get hotter as I descended the Inner Gorge toward the Colorado River.

2. Into the Depths

After a few switchbacks, I met a mountain goat. My spirits were lifted a little by the animal; if only I could walk off the trail and trot almost straight down, as she did as I approached. I did not linger though; I had to get to water and rest my legs some more. I reached the short tunnel just before the black bridge in relatively short time. My legs were begging me to stop but I could not afford to—I even passed the Indian ruins without pausing to read the sign.

I crossed the little bridge over the creek and began to thrill that my travail was almost over. I had made it to the Bright Angel Campground. I spotted a campsite beside the river that looked good—it even had a wooden table on which I could lie stretched out. I threw off my pack and clambered up onto the table. And there I lay in a state akin to rigor mortis—nothing and no one could have made me move.

After about twenty minutes, the table's hardness prompted me to get out my sleeping mat and tent. I swung my legs to the ground and tried to stand up. Searing pain shot through me. I immediately sat back down. And then it occurred to me... yet another mistake: I

119

had no anti-inflammatory medicine. And it was clear that I was not going to be able to walk for a while. I had to get the sleeping mat and give myself more time on top of the table.

I butt-shuffled to the pack, retrieved the mat, rolled it out on the table, and stretched out once more.

It was at this time that a young couple came over to ask me if I needed help. The girl was from Tampa, the guy from Missouri, and they offered to take my water bottles down to the faucet and fill them for me. I thanked them profusely and, on their return, drank until I could drink no more.

After about an hour, a ranger came by. Perhaps he, too, recognized someone in trouble, or maybe the young couple had told him. I sat up, swinging my legs down to the bench, and told him that I was simply "wiped out," that I had carried too much weight, and that, despite my training and planning, I hadn't been prepared for such a long walk with such a big pack. He gave me some pills that he said would help but, after hearing my symptoms, told me that even after a good night's sleep, I would still not be walking easily the next day. I told him I had to load up on water and go back up to Cremation to retrieve the rest of my stuff.

"You brought more than all of this?" he asked.

Sheepishly and somewhat ashamed, I confessed that, yes, I had. Then he told me in no uncertain terms that I would have to stay in the Bright Angel Campground for at least two nights.

I was dismayed. "But what about my stuff on the Tonto, and my itinerary that takes me over to Grapevine and back?" (The Backpacker Reservation Office insists that everyone follows their itinerary to a tee, especially when it involves campgrounds that are "filled every night.")

The ranger's name was Bryan Wisher. He was very nice, very concerned, and took charge. He promised to hike up and get my stuff, and to bring it to me before dark. Then he would rewrite my permit, allowing me to stay an extra night—they always held back one or two emergency openings.

"Are there others as foolish as me, then?" I asked.

He nodded and assured me that I wasn't the first and would surely not be the last. He wrote me up for two nights, followed by one night up at Indian Garden on the Bright Angel Trail, from where I could climb out the next day. He would fetch my gear and I could have the mules carry it out at a dollar per pound—I could make the arrangements the next day, after breakfast. I was too embarrassed to argue, but instead gratefully resigned myself to Wisher's help and the new itinerary. Still thoroughly embarrassed, I thanked him profusely.

I remember thinking that it would not be possible for Wisher to bring my load down before sunset, but he assured me it was no problem and that he was a "fast walker." He seemed happy to have an excuse to "take a short walk." I warned him that I had a lot of stuff up there, since I was planning on a week's trip and had clearly brought way too much. Perhaps, I suggested, I should pick it up myself, later. No, Wisher insisted, he would "run" up the Inner Gorge and come back with my extras. I relented.

He left and, relaxing in the knowledge that I had been saved from my own foolishness, I lay back down and fell asleep on the tabletop.

An hour or so later, I slowly made my way over to my pack, dragged it to the tent site and proceeded to put up the tent as best I could without getting to my feet—a long process. Once the tent was up, I pulled the mat and bag inside and went back to fitful resting. It would be dinner time at Phantom Ranch in a while. I wondered how long it was going to take me to go that quarter of a mile to the canteen. I'd better leave early so I could take my time.

At last, it was time to move. I pulled myself out of the tent and was pleased to find my legs were working a little better. As I was preparing for dinner—a change of shirt and a brief wash-up—Wisher walked past my campsite. He looked in on me, and I asked in astonishment, "You got my stuff already?"

No, he replied, he was just now leaving to get it.

"At this hour?" I asked, incredulous. "It will be dark soon."

He told me not to worry, he was a fast walker and knew the trail well, and off he strode as I, ever so slowly, moved out of my campsite in search of dinner.

I could take about ten steps before I desperately needed a rest. *What the hell did I do to myself?* I focused on one step at a time. I must have used every rock, rail, and bench imaginable on that incredibly slow climb. As I crawl-walked towards Phantom Ranch, I vowed to myself that in the future I would not bring everything suggested in the guidebooks, but just the bare necessities, plus an umbrella and two walking poles. Furthermore, and most importantly, I would plan my trips so that I did not have to carry a heavy pack for more than 4 or 5 miles a day. After all, my object was to enjoy the beauty, to soak up the solitude and silence, and to reflect on life, not pretend I was the kid I once was, or some athlete in top condition. I told myself that it did not matter how many mistakes we made in life, but rather, how much we learned from them.

I made it to the tables outside the canteen and joined others already there waiting for the dinner bell to sound. Only then did I realize that I was very hungry. But first I wanted to use the payphone to call my wife. I dialed the number and waited. As I did so, I found my breathing deepen and lengthen as I relaxed—it was a very nice evening, about 75 degrees, with a slight wind, and I was going to survive.

Donna answered, "I miss you so."

I told her of my troubles, but reassured her that Wisher had saved me and that I had learned not to take chances or try to do more than I should. She told me that at home they were being buffeted by a rare March Nor'easter. We wished each other safe and said our goodbyes.

I sat and waited for dinner. I thought about Donna in our house in the storm, the wind flexing the large plate-glass windows as it swept ashore; the rain and snow driving *up* the glass and the side of the house. The snow plastering everything outside, the branches that would bring down power lines and plunge her world into darkness and cold. Then I thought about Donna sitting in the dark, wondering why in the world I had to hike by myself in the Grand Canyon. I would try (but no doubt fail) to explain, because even then, with my aching legs and dehydrated body, I knew I would be back, time and again, determined to take on the canyon until I "got it right."

The dinner bell rang, and I went in to eat. Despite my aching legs and back, I smiled and tried to be "chirpy." I ate a very good meal and offered silent thanks for Bryan Wisher.

After eating, I went out and sat on the benches. I took out my notebook and wrote, "I soon will be home, dear Donna, with a new appreciation of you."

I returned to camp, moving more easily, but certainly not close to being ready to backpack again. I had used the bathrooms at the Ranch, so was ready to crawl into bed and let sleep take over. But, when I made it back to my site, there was all my extra stuff sitting on the picnic table. Wisher had retrieved it, going out and back in about the time it had taken me to crawl to dinner, call home, eat, and walk back. That guy must be something on the trails! I did not know then that Bryan Wisher was a legendary rescuer in the Grand Canyon and that his calm confidence came not from bravado but from experience.

As I tucked myself into my sleeping bag, I laughed at myself once more. Everything looks doable on the map, but the reality is a different story. How could I have been so foolish? After everything I had been through on Grandview, how could I have fallen into yet another disaster? Then I realized: there was a direct correlation between my growing over-confidence and the number of new equipment purchases. All those new-fangled gadgets and toys had been my downfall. All I really needed was the old-fashioned coffee pot that could double as a water boiling pot for my dehydrated meals, and one aluminum cup that could serve as both cup and bowl. Instead, I had brought two pots, two powerful and heavy flashlights, back-up batteries, *and* candles... Well, no more. From now on there would be one head lamp for emergency night walking, and a few back-up candles. I had even brought a small hammer to pound in the tent stakes, but any flat rock would have done. And so my thoughts ran on.

As a philosopher, I was familiar with the motif of modern hubris created by the feeling of apparent technological superiority over nature. As good as my new backpack was, I was no match for the Kaibab trail and the 75lb weight. I could, of course, have blamed the Bright Angel Lodge for not providing scales in my room, but I would not get into the "blame game" or the comfort of scapegoating. No, the fault was mine. I was the fool. I had screwed up, but maybe next time I would get it right.

The east side of the Bright Angel Campground runs along the creekside, about 20ft from the edge. At night, as the campers settle in, the soothing noise of the stream and the river beyond calm the mind and promote sleep. As I drifted off, my mind raced over the day and beyond.

I remembered once reading the words of Black Elk to my students in my class on Native American Religion, held in Boston Public Garden. Black Elk experienced shamanic travel into the clouds, where he saw many apocalyptic images. It was hot that Boston day, and I was sitting in the sun, worrying about a reoccurrence of the melanoma I had had in my early thirties. Apparently, and quite contrary to my intentions, I was giving some of my students the impression of an "otherness," a strange, fascinating realm of far away, exotic mentality and experience quite separate from the usual bourgeois world they knew. Every American teenager has a thirst for such an experience sooner or later. For some, the yearning manifests in tattoos, others will follow a guru or take up yoga, some study Eastern religions or follow some crazed rocker, and still others lose themselves in a wilderness experience.

Undoubtedly, many of my students took my Native American Religion class or my Philosophy of Nature class for that very reason. They were looking for the Faustian experience, erotic and worldly success at the cost of giving up the care of soul. I tried to teach that "the other" was simply that which we failed to see in our own lives, that it had to be "demythologized," rather than projected into some un-real fantasy world that brings on delusions. In short, all religions—from the earliest shamanism to contemporary Protestant religions, such as Unitarianism—are about the human unconscious, what Carl Jung called "the collective unconscious." Jung, and others after him, knew that all religious experience is critically important, but only when the account of such experience is not literalized. Within the human unconscious lies enormous powers, but if these powers are transferred from that unconscious directly into the human ego, the result is "psychic inflation."

The Greeks knew this (although even Plato never fully demythologized Greek religion) and created the legend of Daedalus and Icarus. Daedalus made wings of wax and feathers—a pair for himself, another for his son, Icarus. As he gave the wings to the young man, he admonished him to take care, not to fly too low where the damp would clog the feathers, nor too high, where the sun would melt the wax that held everything together.

Of course, this story has nothing to do with ascending into the air. Rather, the lesson is that the human psyche must practice a balancing act—neither too unconscious ("low") nor too conscious ("high"), in the sense of psychic inflation—what is often called "egoism" or "egotism." The legend of Icarus follows to its inevitable finale: Icarus is enticed by the sun, flies too near it, and crashes to the ground, as the sun's heat melts his wings. He has learned the lesson, but at the cost of his life.

The other lesson to be gleaned from the story is that hubris leads to a fall if we are not guided by the archetype of the Father, whose wisdom needs to be taken into the youth's soul. Icarus would not heed his father and the consequences were fatal.

The "ups" and "downs" of mythology and all religion (even religion that is historicized) are metaphors and symbols, not to be taken literally. The Grand Canyon is geographically very low but can be experientially very "high"—people often say they experience the

125

greatest high of their life within the Grand Canyon. For myself, I had learned from my Grandview attempt and now, my trip to Phantom Ranch, that I needed to stay in a state of balance. In real terms, I needed to stay on the Tonto Plateau, literally the middle level between the depths of the Colorado River and the heights of the North and South Rims. Canyon topography correlated with psychological wisdom.

In *Thus Spake Zarathustra*, Nietzsche pointed to the "ceiling truth." We must retreat from the Faustian thrust and look down closely at our own pasts to find that shamanic part of our otherwise very "ordinary" lives. Now, as I lay in my tent, approaching sleep, it suddenly occurred to me: I was producing a charismatic figure for myself *vis-à-vis* my students. Previously, I had discussed the good and bad aspects of charisma in my classes, and now I was concocting both in myself. I determined to take Daedalus's admonition to heart as I continued my professorship, and go neither too high, nor too low. Furthermore, I vowed to use charisma sparingly and carefully. With that, I returned to the process of going to sleep.

But sleep was elusive and, as I often do when focusing on relaxing, I reached for an "orientation." I was at the bottom of a side canyon to a great gorge on a planet that was miraculously situated at the optimum distance from its star, with a moon stabilizing the wobble of its axis, and a large gaseous planet (Jupiter) beyond its orbit gobbling up dangerous solar debris. As I marveled at the interconnectivity of life, I arrived at the point of being able to say: "all is *entangled, ensnared, enamored*"—to use Nietzsche's description. I had looked up "enamored" when first reading that section of *Zarathustra*. It means "to inflame with love"; "ensnared" suggests luck, and "entangled" reflects the oft-overlooked fact of life that good and evil are entangled, the "good" often being not so good, and the "evil" sometimes leading to a good outcome. Jung believed that each archetype of the unconscious has the potential for either good or evil, depending on how consciousness relates to the archetypes.

As I fell into sleep, I chuckled at how my mind was wandering through my life, and how it was all so certainly "entangled." Nietzsche was right, to love life means to wish that everything, the good and the bad, would return. The wish, the desire, creates the eternal life, and the result is "the will to power," inner power, that of character (see James Hillman, *The Force of Character* [Random House, 1999]).

I certainly was "ensnared" at the mouth of Bright Angel Canyon—immobile, in pain, humbled, but alive. I thought how a teacher, any *real* teacher, becomes entangled in his/her culture, in his/her students, in his/her ideas. Then I noticed that the pain in my legs was diminishing, or perhaps I had distanced myself from it. At last, I fell into a deep sleep.

3. The Yucca Cache and a Ranger's Compassion

Bryan Wisher had gone up the Kaibab to the top of the Gorge and found my cache in the yucca clump. He had come back down as it was getting dark, and, as he told me the next day, he had fallen, the first time he had done so, and injured himself. At that time, I knew nothing about Bryan Wisher, except that he was being very nice to me and very professional.

Apart from the inconvenience of retrieving my kit, I had also worried that when he found it, he'd have trouble getting hold of it. I had planted everything in the very middle of the yucca bush, assuming that the only human "intruder" would be me. It had never occurred to me that I might be putting someone else in harm's way.

My chosen hiding place was a banana yucca (*yucca baccata*), known for its fruit, which is green, but shaped like a small banana, and develops in late April into May. I was there in March, and the center of the plant was empty, since the stalk had yet to form, and thus perfect for my storage. All yuccas are part of the agave family and all, especially the banana yucca, are used by the Navaho for ceremonially cleansing and making ceremonial masks.

There are four principal Grand Canyon plant communities,

depending on the elevation and location: white fir forest on the North Rim, Ponderosa pine and pinyon/juniper woodland on the South, blackbrush on the Tonto, and desert scrub in the Inner Canyon.

Then there are the more individual species, such as the Utah juniper, an example of which is the magnificent tree just north of the new Grand Canyon National Park headquarters on the rim Trail; the century plant, noticed only when it sends up its flower stalk about once every twenty-five years; the banana and narrow-leaf yuccas, also seldom noticed unless in bloom. In the Inner Gorge, one finds the creosote bush and saltbush, along with associates such as mesquite, various cacti, and the catclaw acacia, whose name comes from its ability to grab hold of the backpacker's hat or pack as he makes his way through the Monument campground. There is also an acacia at Horn Creek's one and only designated camp spot. The sacred datura (a member of the nightshade family) has large, white, tubular flowers of 6-10in, looks somewhat like a lily, and blooms at night; it is very poisonous to humans and should not be touched. Along the Colorado there is another class of plants dominated by the Fremont cottonwood, and the invasive, foreign tamarisk.

In a semi-arid desert, as found on the Tonto Trail, plants stand out from the rock and are thus more dramatic. I am fascinated by the fact that hemlock seedlings will take hold on the top of rocks, using dust, debris, and decomposing hemlock leaves as their only soil, until they can find a roothold within cracks of the rock—they will often send roots around the rock, no matter how large. Finally, once sufficient nutrients are found, they grow as if the rock were not even there.

Appalachian trails are covered with roots, and surrounded by forests of hemlock, birch, beech, poplar, and occasionally pine. When fall arrives, the leaves cascade down onto the trail and, after a rain, become as slippery as snow or ice. By contrast, in the Grand Canyon there are no roots, no excessive vegetation—even among the cottonwoods—no recurring violent weather, no bugs (mosquitoes or black flies), and no water-logged trails.

The exception to this last aspect is in the deep and/or narrow ("slot") canyons, where water can present very real and very sudden issues. A canyon whose walls are so sheer that they are unclimbable except with technical equipment is, essentially, a drainpipe. Imagine the rim of the Grand Canyon as the roof of your house. When it rains the water rushes off the roof into the gutter, the drainage basin below. From there the gutter feeds into the drainpipe and thence, eventually into the catch basin—the Colorado River. The force of the original rainfall high up on the rims may be minimal, but as the water accumulates and concentrates, and as the gradient down which it flows sharpens dramatically, the result is a force of such magnitude that it can move boulders larger than cars, large tree trunks, and incredible amounts of mud. And all this water and debris and power flow into and through the slot canyons.

The rangers are very familiar with this "water-channeling phenomenon." They know it as one of the most dangerous aspects for hikers in the Grand Canyon and, along with simply falling from the edge when taking pictures, heat exhaustion and stroke, flash floods account for many of the canyon's deaths—a storm occurring 30 or 40 miles away may kill a person hiking in a side canyon.

In *Over the Edge: Death in the Grand Canyon*, authors Michael Ghiglieri and Thomas Myers write about the flash flood of March 5, 1995, a "mere" twenty-nine years after the super-flood of 1966 in Crystal Creek. Crystal Creek drains a huge area, made up of the confluence of Crystal and Dragon Creek with the Hindu Amphitheater towering above. Dragon also drains Little Dragon and Milk Creek, and the head drainage area of these creeks penetrates miles north of the Grand Canyon Lodge. Crystal itself has a dozen main feeder streams, and in hard rains, many others materialize as the water falls from 8,100ft into the drainages some 2,500ft below.

The head drainage of Bright Angel Creek is perhaps a quarter of the size of Crystal's, but Bright Angel Creek picks up the Transept Creek, Manzanita Creek, as well as the Uncle Jim area and the Roaring Springs area, where the North Kaibab climbs out to the North Rim. More importantly, the Bright Angel Creek penetrates above the rim all the way to the edge of the start of the Nankoweap Trail, which is even north of the head of Crystal. To make matters worse, Phantom Creek dumps into Bright Angel Creek in an opening through the towering rock wall, which is not apparent until one is right on top of it.

The mouth of Phantom Creek may be only 20ft across, perhaps less, and Phantom Canyon is a slot canyon reaching back toward Isis Temple before it opens out to Haunted Canyon and back beyond Isis, where it drains the east side of the ridge that separates Phantom from the Trinity drainage. In times of heavy rainfall, all the water west of Bright Angel roars down the Phantom slot canyon and dumps into the Bright Angel Creek—in a state of flood it will tear up the trail and slam into the east wall of the Box—the narrow portion of the Bright Angel Canyon in which Phantom Ranch is located.

On the night of March 5, 1995, heavy rain fell on the North Rim and employees sleeping in the bungalow at Phantom Ranch were awoken by a terrible roar from the Bright Angel Creek. Many of them went down the east side of the canyon to view the immense confluence. Within minutes, they were stranded on an island as the flood waters rose and cut them off from safety.

Bryan Wisher was stationed at Indian Garden that night and was summoned for help at 1:00 a.m. He recruited another man and they started down the Bright Angel Trail alongside the swollen Garden Creek in the dark and the pouring rain. Myers and Ghiglieri write that "Wisher's rib hurt with each step." When I read the passage for the first time, my heart sank. It was while retrieving my gear from the yucca plant on the Tonto Trail that Wisher had fallen and injured his rib. That had been just a few short years before the flood—had my carelessness contributed to his discomfort?

Time and again one hears that the Grand Canyon is potentially a very dangerous place, frequently underestimated by modern visitors. The rescues that the rangers accomplish are often miraculous and always heroic. Myers and Ghiglieri do justice to many of them in *Over the Edge: Death in Grand Canyon,* and I don't believe anyone should hike the Grand Canyon before reading it.

The authors have three theories about why so many deaths or near-deaths occur in the Grand Canyon. They outline their first in the foreword:

> Despite the obvious dangers of Grand Canyon, a frequent observation I have made of many visitors is their tendency to have a "911 mentality." They often make the assumption that help will always be immediately forthcoming when they place themselves in harm's way. Such visitors suffer from the misguided belief that a national park is a close cousin to an amusement park. The realities are that Walt Disney did not have a hand in constructing Grand Canyon, and the inherent risks associated with this park are unbelievably real. And all too often, tragically so.

The average American has no first-hand experience of real life-threatening danger unless they have an accident. But all of us can have the pseudo-experience of being scared by a movie, a video game, or an amusement-park ride. The ordinary signals that come to us when in danger have been blunted by these "Disney" experiences, so that they are ignored or never even reach the brain's decision-making centers. If one never experiences real danger, one cannot learn from it, and thus will never make the mistakes that are so important to improving our skills and abilities. Many will not know to be careful until it is too late.

Added to our own ambivalence and invincibility, our equipment becomes ever more sophisticated and, as it does so, our knowledge and respect for dangerous activities diminish. We are led to believe that the latest technology will see us right and, if it fails, there will be someone to rescue us.

Myers and Ghiglieri's second theory can be termed "the lottery of death" mentality:

> Downstream, the mouth of Havasu looked like a typical summer traffic jam. For river guides, the apparently dry "holes" during the monsoons

are tempting. After all, their emotional logic runs, we're here, and it doesn't look like rain, and some of my passengers may never be here again. ...let's hike it, at least a short way up. Again, the "lottery of death" mentality nudges people into decisions to hike slot canyons that later may seem a lot less smart.

—ibid.

But, in this example, the passengers are being taken for a ride by "experts" who are supposed to keep them safe. What is overlooked is that the mule and boat rides in the Grand Canyon—the two ways that most of the public experience the canyon below the rims—have turned the park into "just another" amusement park. Running the rapids is inherently the type of life-threatening activity that gives one the feeling of somehow having conquered nature, of a sort of "immortality." The danger signals are blunted once more; "someone will pull me out of the river if I am thrown; the stats of successful runs versus deaths are very good, after all."

The fact of the matter is that in a real adventure, one does not go looking for trouble; on the contrary, one does everything one can to be safe. A real thrill is quite different and much better than the artificial thrill experienced on "rides."

The disconnect from reality is not unique to the Grand Canyon. In 1999, 287 million people visited the country's national parks, and 4,603 of them had to be rescued, while 211 died from falls, drownings, or other "accidents." In 1996, visitors to the Grand Canyon *alone* required 482 searches and rescues, and eighteen people died (that were reported). Most visitors stay in areas where the trails are excellent and there are plenty of experienced people around to help in an emergency. And yet, some eighteen deaths and many more near-deaths continue to occur every year.

The authors' third theory is that of "the solo hiker mistake," as targeted by George Steck, a Grand Canyon hiking expert, when he said: "A solo hiker often has a fool for a companion." Meyer and Ghiglieri put it thus: "If you don't possess your own Jiminy Cricket, hike with a companion." I interpret this to mean if you don't have an inner voice capable of putting on the brakes or promoting caution, then don't go alone.

Over the Edge has tables listing deaths in the Grand Canyon, and the first two, "Accidental Lethal Falls from rims of the Grand Canyon" and "Environmental Deaths within the Grand Canyon" carry within their descriptions the distinction of **solo** trips. However, the study of each indicates something other than the simple confirmation of the authors' third theory. Here are some examples:

> Mystery Man, adult, March, 1900: Upper Granite Gorge about 300ft above the river near river mile 91. Skeleton of a likely **solo hiker**. Apparent hypothermia/exhaustion scenario of tourist or hob-nail booted prospector 2+ miles off the beaten track. No traumatic injury evident.

> Bennie Tohe, 72, June 23, 1960: Beamer Trail near River Mile 65, about two miles upstream of the Tanner Trail and only 25 yards from the Colorado River. Tohe, a Navajo medicine man from the Chinle area, was **solo hiking** back from having visited the confluence of the Colorado and Little Colorado rivers on a private quest/pilgrimage (the confluence is a sacred area for Navajos). While well-hydrated and leaving firm footprints spaced at a healthy pace, Tohe died suddenly of heat-related cardiac arrest at a temperature of 114 degrees in the shade.

When one is going solo, there is no question that one must be extra careful: take a snake-bite kit, a whistle, a water pump with floating end, etc. But, as far as I know, not one solo *backpacker* has died in the Grand Canyon; Myers and Ghiglieri's third theory applies to solo hikers, not backpackers.

It was the morning after my first night at Bright Angel campground. I had slept intermittently, still with sore legs and back. And now, as I started up the campground middle walk, I was amazed at how stiff and sore my legs still felt. But, I told myself, I had all day and another night to recover before leaving for Indian Garden (my new itinerary), so I must take it easy, even if I was late to breakfast. One of the reasons I had decided to go all the way to the Bright Angel Creek, even after my legs were "killing me" on my first day, was because I could get dinner and breakfast there without carrying the food.

Now, as I moved slowly and stiffly up towards the ranch canteen, I knew that Wisher was right, I must stay and rest.

The meals at Phantom Ranch are served on long tables, perhaps fifteen or more places on each side, and large bowls of food are handed down the table from the end nearest the kitchen. For the previous night's dinner, we had had a choice of steak, beef stew, or vegetarian loaf. I had chosen the beef stew, rich in both protein and carbs. By the time I had arrived for the meal, there was but one open seat next to a woman who was a trail guide in the Rockies. She had a nervous habit of moving her knee up and down rapidly, her toes keeping it in constant motion, and even as she had fidgeted, she had talked non-stop about how many miles she and her companions had walked that day. After a while I'd found I could tolerate the constant movement, but the bragging was getting under my skin.

As I approached the dining room for breakfast, I realized I was fifteen minutes late and, once again, there was but one open seat. It was next to the same woman. She and her companions had already devoured all the bacon and pancakes, and for some reason they had also taken my plate, a fact that one of them acknowledged with a laugh: "I didn't know you were coming."

I inwardly groaned. Was there to be no breakfast after all? But I needn't have worried. Despite my late arrival, the staff rustled up bacon, eggs, and pancakes and I ate in peace, as the other hikers had eaten and departed.

I signed up and paid for the evening's dinner and headed off for my day of leg reclamation. My legs were improving and already feeling remarkably better than they had on the way up through the campground. Clearly what I needed to do was rest, while lightly exercising. And so, I spent the rest of that day walking around, never going far, never fast, and never with my backpack.

It was an otherwise unremarkable day. My breakfast had been so large that I had no need of lunch, but dug into some trail mix while contemplating the power of water to slice through the towering cliffs of Bright Angel. I ate a second hearty dinner and enjoyed another good night's sleep beside the creek.

And with that, the next morning arrived. I delivered my excess load to the mule depot outside the canteen, paid my dollar per pound to have it carried out, consumed another large breakfast, and set off for Indian Garden. It was an uneventful and very enjoyable walk. The trail parallels first the Pipe Springs Creek and then the Garden Creek. I took my time up through the Devil's corkscrew, stopping frequently along the way. My legs had recovered pretty much, but I was in no hurry. I ate various granola bars and trail mix, and arrived at Indian Garden in the early afternoon, braced for another evening among tourists.

4. Indian Garden: Creek Cracks and Mulish Water

The missionaries go forth to Christianize the savages—as if the savages weren't dangerous enough already."

—Edward Abbey: *A Voice Crying in the Wilderness: Notes From a Secret Journal* (St. Martin's Griffin, 1989).

Indian Garden was historically farmed by the Havasupa until they were told by Teddy Roosevelt, personally, that they must leave immediately because he had declared the Grand Canyon a national monument. The area was successfully cultivated by the tribe, thanks to a natural spring just below and to the west of today's campground. Most of the year the Indian Garden creek is dry upstream from the camp but below the spring, water runs continuously all the way to Pipe Creek, which is, in turn, fed by a second less abundant spring.

This natural water source also explains why the cottonwoods grow so profusely at Indian Garden.

As one approaches Indian Garden from the Inner Gorge, one comes first to a corral and horse shed—the creek flowing just east of them—with benches and a Multrum toilet. This is the resting place for visitors ascending and descending by mule and six or so mule trains tie up to rest and eat here each day.

I arrived in the early afternoon of Monday, March 15, 1992, made my way through the corral, and found, to my delight, that the only tent site that stands away from the smell and noise of the animals was mine for the taking. I strode over, set down my backpack and, after raising my tent and establishing my presence by placing my pot on the table, walked out to Plateau Point for the sunset. There were few clouds, so little red in the sky, but the play of shadows on the buttes, temples, and rocky outcrops was enchanting.

I returned from my sojourn to find that I had been joined by a scout leader. He was intent on offering me his poor opinion of the Backcountry Reservation Office, yet I was unable to follow the gist of his complaint. As he talked, I couldn't help wondering about his troop setting up camp next door. There were about a dozen or so boys and I was tempted to ask their talkative leader if he knew there were specific sites for larger parties. I did not… I have never minded the noise of children and I saw no need to complain.

A couple from British Columbia camped down quietly on the other side of me. All was well in my world. In my notebook that evening I wrote: "How delicious the night! Warm desert winds reminiscent of Palm Springs. The winds turn on, then off, as they sweep up the canyon, the usual pattern created by colder air from the rim sinking down to replace the heated air of the cliffs rising up." I had clearly, almost totally, recovered physically and was at last enjoying the beauty of my surroundings.

I wondered about the layout of Indian Garden. The tent sites are, with the exception of Number 7, where I was, close together and close to the comings and goings of the mule trains and their tourists. Clearly aware of this, the rangers were stationed some distance above the campgrounds, where it was both quieter and removed from the hustle and bustle. It seemed to me that the mules had a pretty prime position, which perhaps they didn't need, and that if the shed and corral were moved to the east hillside, their manure would not run off into and pollute the Indian Garden Creek. Then the toilets, west of the campground, could be moved to the current mule shed location, the corral area could be planted with new cottonwoods, and the campground could be extended down to the creek. By doing this, I reckoned, a further twenty designated campsites could be established all along the creek.

But such plans would have to wait. For now, I was content to be without pain and to be once more engaging with nature and all its beauty.

5. Horn Creek: Taking Note

I was up at the crack of dawn, quietly took my tent down and packed up, and was out on the Tonto West trail heading toward Horn Creek within fifteen minutes—I would wait and have breakfast once the sun hit the trail. From Indian Garden it is only 2.5 miles of gentle trail to Horn Creek. I forded Indian Garden Creek, took the trail toward Plateau Point, and then turned onto the Tonto West trail. I had only ever *crossed* Tonto West trail and was thrilled to be walking along it. It was a beautiful spring morning, my legs were finally like new, and the pack, thanks to Bryan Wisher and the mules from Phantom Ranch, was 30lb lighter and bearable. I was looking forward to a night of solitary camping at Horn Creek before heading back to Indian Garden for more water and thence the 4.5-mile ascent up the Bright Angel Trail and back to "civilization."

After my two nights at Bright Angel Creek and one at Indian Garden, it would be nice to be alone again.

I rounded the Battleship, followed the west ridge of Bright Angel Canyon, and approached the Horn Creek chasm before the trail turned south and toward the head of the creek's cut into the Tonto. The Tonto Plateau is so benign here that my mind wandered, but, I reminded myself, I was alone now and should pay attention, particularly in the early morning when I might meet a rattlesnake. Nevertheless, I did feel like celebrating. I was out of the Inner Corridor, away from the tourists, and finally "on my own." I took a brief rest, swallowed a mouthful of trail gorp and a gulp of water, and looked around.

Right then and there I promised myself that I would return. I would learn from my many mistakes, would do Horn to Hermit on my own and return to the South Rim via Bright Angel Trail—there would be no more Bright Angel or Indian Garden campgrounds for me. They had served me well, but I would not be needing them next time. I walked on with a spring in my step.

After a series of gullies, I descended a small slope and arrived at the junction of trail and creek bed. It was still only 8:45 a.m. when I found the perfect camping spot beneath a couple of acacia trees, and about 6ft from the trickle of the creek. This was the east branch of Horn Creek. The west branch was just over the rise and about an eighth of a mile further on. Together, the two branches drain the area between the Battleship to the west and the 5,036ft Dana Butte, named after geologist James Wright Dana (1813–1895), to the east.

I took off my backpack, set it against a large rock, pulled out my ground cloth and leaned back to take in my surroundings. The points of Hopi and Maricopa, with the Powell Memorial between them, were straight up and over my head. Through the eons, Horn Creek has created an amphitheater, with the little Horn Creek campsite as the podium on the stage. The two branches of Horn Creek meet just north of the camping spot, where a protruding flat rock on top of the cliff allows for a good scenic overlook. I decided I should go and explore this at some point, but for now I wanted nothing more than to soak in the glorious morning and settle in for a day of pure leisure.

Usually, when I'm backpacking, I write short notes in my trail notebook, a few words, or abbreviations. But on this trip, I had written even less than usual and, while recovering in Bright Angel Campground, had written barely a word. Now, on my first full day and night in isolation, I had the impulse to write more. Thus, as I settled into my stay at Horn Creek I wrote:

> There must be a lesson in the creek's apparent fragility and diminution, yet its work product is all around us. A gentle, slow flow of water down the gradient of life's overall landscape works tremendous results, if only given enough time. Such time comes to one in the last stage of life.

Ten years later, with the images of Horn Creek and its campsite still vivid in my mind, I added:

> I've been cutting deeper and deeper for "eons" of human time [forty years or so] with a broad and deep chasm beginning to open out, but no traveler has ventured with me, as yet. Perchance my fate is to be one of those endless but tremendous canyons that no one has ever seen. Do human eyes, those connected to any old brain, consecrate such a canyon? Or does its sheer facticity suffice? And for what? All I can do now is flow down my canyon—at sixty, it has taken its course and does not allow for trailblazing to other places. So cut deep and don't worry—glory in one's own activity, as Horn Creek apparently does. The hawk and squirrel and occasional goat know of thee, and compared with the specialized brain of man, they stand taller. But of the soul, the maker of canyons like these creeks, perhaps such soul is in all of us, even as in this stone and water.

I was in wonder of my own inner journey, but thought that surely all humans experience some version of it. I did not want my ego to carry me away; soul makes canyons in our psyche, and one's soul is somewhat in opposition to one's ego, even if the daemon is always ready to bring them together. If my life was cutting a deep canyon within, so be it. Life is what happens to you; it is not the outcome of a scheme or plan. It is what it is, and we should embrace it, as Nietzsche did when he wished its return.

When I awoke the next day, the sun was yet to peek over The Battleship. I watched it as it crept down the hill across the creek from the rock on which I was sitting. It stole into the amphitheater and shortened the tails of the butte's shadows. It was to be another grand day in the canyon. As John Muir would say, "what an honor and privilege to be alive with all this."

I followed my routine day: up at dawn, load up and get on the trail, in this case the ascent of the Bright Angel Trail. After stocking up on clean water, I crossed Indian Garden and moved on up to Jacob's Ladder before the sun hit me hard.

The hike out was uneventful. After "topping out," I climbed into a taxi to take me back to my rental car at the Kaibab trailhead. In comparison to my week of walking, the taxi flew across the pavement, and I'm sure I hung on for dear life.

It had been another largely unsuccessful trip, and yet I was full of life and content in the knowledge that I would, unquestionably, be back the following year.

Hikers looking down on a long, fairly straight stretch of the
Colorado River. *Photo by Gary Ladd*

CHAPTER 5

MONUMENT CANYON TRANSFORMATION

Side Canyons

. . . .

1. Slot Canyon Intrusion

2. Hermit Without Paper

3. The Ecstasy of Monument Creek: Panology

4. Nature Deficit Disorder

At 8:00 p.m., March 13, 1993, and I was at the Bright Angel Lodge. It had been a long and arduous journey from the East Coast, but I was excited to be back in the Grand Canyon. I felt experienced and prepared for the solo trek ahead. I settled into my room, got to sleep late, and woke early.

I was impatient to get going and, before breakfast, decided to go down to the Bright Angel Trailhead to check out the conditions. For the first 100ft or so, even this early on a cold morning, it appeared to be ice-free. Satisfied that things looked about as good as I could have hoped, I went back up to the café, ate a hearty breakfast, and then called Donna. Everything is fine, I told her, I'll be heading out soon. This would be the last communication between us for a week—there were no phones on the Tonto West trail, and the cell phone was still a thing of the future. My itinerary, I told her, although she probably knew it by heart, was Indian Garden, Salt, Monument and/or Hermit, back to Monument, Salt, Horn, and back up the Bright Angel Trail.

By 9:30 a.m. I was back at the trailhead.

Bright Angel Trail is wide—as wide as 5ft or even 8ft in many places—but I was carrying a load, even if less than I had carried last year, so I was determined that, no matter how easy the trail, I would take it slow. I had two poles, and an umbrella lashed to my Terraplane backpack. I had learned by experience, and experience leads to exploration.

And so I began my next Grand Canyon adventure, alone again with the rocks, the trail, and my thoughts.

Just a few feet down the trail I ran into ice, lots of ice. I was shocked. Apparently, my earlier reconnaissance had missed that the trail was covered by a mix of mule dung and dirt that obscured a layer of sheet ice beneath. Not only that, but the combination of dung and rock dust had created an insulating blanket that kept the ice frozen longer than in other parts of the canyon. Not for the first time I found myself cursing the mules. I wondered if others saw them as the enemy. But there was nothing to be done. As my friend Kim Crumbo said: "the mules are all about money for the Park, so they come first."

After just a few steps, I knew I had to go for the crampons. I had brought some with me but hadn't really expected to use them. I had to take off my 55lb backpack, lean it against a trailside rock, and struggle to get the crampons on. Within the next quarter mile, they fell off three times. They were almost as maddening as the mules!

I had not used the crampons on ice before, although I had practiced on snow around the house, primarily to get used to the tricky strapping arrangements. It seemed improbable to be staking my life on two steel triangles protruding from the middle of my boot, all the while praying that they would cut into the ice and hold me, a 215lb man with a 55lb pack, on the trail. The drop-offs at the beginning of Bright Angel Trail are straight down for hundreds, if not a thousand feet or more, and in some places there is nothing to grab hold of as you slip. The combination of ice, crampons that would not stay put, and that sheer drop kept me focused.

There are four landmark points on the early part of the Bright Angel Trail—two tunnels, and then two rest houses. The second rest house, at 3 miles in, has an emergency phone and stretcher. After that comes Jacob's Ladder, a series of reddish switchbacks, and a much easier section, with no more ice, less frightening drop-offs, and no more mules.

I had walked very slowly on the top part of the trail, but once the crampons were no longer needed and I could move more confidently, I began to relax. Nevertheless, I was still cautious, reminding myself that my pack made me top-heavy, and to follow my number one rule: "stop walking before looking at the scenery, and stop looking when you start walking again." It is a discipline that requires some practice but undoubtedly saves lives.

It was early afternoon by the time I reached Indian Garden, but the spot closest to the cottonwoods where I had stayed last year was still unoccupied. I washed the mule dung off my crampons with the Roaring Springs water pumped into a fountain at the top of the campground, set up the tent, organized my pack, and relaxed. Despite the ice, it had been a good start and I was pleased with my progress. But the head cold that I had been ignoring since leaving home, combined with the lingering fatigue from the journey, persuaded me not to walk out to Plateau Point or Pipe Springs. I would go to bed early and get a good night's sleep.

By 5:30 p.m., the campground was still half empty, and the ranger had yet to make the rounds—I found myself hoping it would not be Bryan Wisher; I had no wish to revisit the embarrassment of our previous encounter.

I made up my cache for Horn—two canteens of Roaring Springs water, the smaller fuel bottle, one dinner plus trail mix, and my crampons. I had decided to go out on the Tonto West trail to Hermit and then return via the same route. There were several places on the way where I could cache supplies and thus reduce my load. Monument had year-round water, but it was a distance between there and Horn, so storing water half-way would help considerably.

So, I settled down in my sleeping bag, and I started mentally designing a proposed house in Sedona (I am yet to build it!). Such imaginings have always contented and calmed me at the end of a day and, sure enough, once I was warm and snug, I drifted off to sleep.

By 7:25 a.m. the following morning I was stepping onto Tonto West and, fifteen minutes later, the sun hit me just in front of The Battleship. I stopped to put on my gaiters. The trail was narrowing and I didn't want the blackbrush to scratch my lower legs. The guidebooks had warned me of this problem, and I was prepared. It was going to be a good day.

The silence was delicious, the day was beautiful—clear skies and about 70 degrees. When I came to the first small tributary, really just a small gulley, I followed its west side out to a flat rock that overlooked the confluence of the two main Horn tributaries. Because of my previous time here, I knew where I was going. I put my first cache in the ledges just before the drop-off, and made a trail note so I could find it on my return.

I crossed the West Horn bed at 9:30 a.m., took out my umbrella, large water bottle, and powder for my feet. I had learned to hike in short boots with mesh tops to keep my feet somewhat cool. I had tried moleskins to prevent blisters but had concluded that regular application of powder and/or water was the best way to keep my toes pain-free. I cached another water bottle and set off again.

Before long I encountered a couple of spots where I was walking within a few feet of the edge of Horn Canyon—a misstep here could have been fatal. The trail was flat, fortunately, but there was nothing between trail and edge to grab hold of before one tumbled into space. Such an exposure would, no doubt, mean little to the pros—indeed I wondered if they would even label it as such—but it made me anxious. But being alone, it didn't matter if I was timid—no need to look cool when no one's looking!

By 10:45 a.m. I was in the small canyon I had dubbed "No-Name Canyon." There was no camping spot, so I decided to leave another cache in some rocks. I made it a rule not to cache close to a camping spot—designated or makeshift—since I believed that the only animal that might possibly disturb my supplies would be a human. For caches I have always wrapped food in two layers of plastic bags, tied tightly, and then put the bags within larger, hard plastic food containers. The pack rats can't smell it and can't nibble through the hard plastic to get at the plastic bags. They *can* chew through a backpack, as I learned years earlier when I found two holes in my pack.

The trail out of No-Name jogged to the northeast, toward the Inner Gorge. It followed the old trail made by the wild burros and seemed to meander unnecessarily. I was tempted to leave it and cut straight across the west flank of Dana Butte, heading due west. But caution won the day and I stayed on course: maybe the burros knew a thing or two. Sure enough, after a half mile I could see the Butte's sides steepen to my left as the trail swung south toward Salt and came close to the edge of the rim. If I had tried my shortcut, I would have had to come down that steep slope, where with one stumble I could have rolled over the trail and into the side canyon.

I paused to take stock and look around me, at the schist on the north side of the Inner Canyon to my right, and the widened mouth of Salt Canyon to my left. Both were frightening chasms; it was time to pay attention. I chuckled to myself. The wild mules were right— stick to the circular route around Dana Butte.

My New England cold was still with me, and I decided that if it were no better the next morning, I would not go beyond Salt. My body was not as young as it once was, and besides, I was also experiencing some digestive issues, no doubt because of the change in diet, and was feeling the weight of my pack. I thought of Harvey Butchart (1907–2002), who had solo-hiked all over the Grand Canyon, always on the move, up, down, sideways, always carrying little weight, never sleeping overnight. His method was "hit and run"—very different from my own, which involved no hitting and absolutely no running. My goal was always to get up at dawn, walk almost casually to the next site, and then spend the afternoon unwinding and musing, conquering nothing but perhaps a few philosophical enigmas!

As I finished my early lunch, I reflected on what I had seen of the

Tonto Trail. From the rim, the Tonto *appeared* to be flat but, in fact, it consisted of a lot of ups and downs in relatively short distances, coupled with lots of ins and outs as one navigated side canyons of side canyons. Abstractly, I had known that this would be the nature of the trail, but it had meant little until I was actually there. Experience is everything; abstract theory without experience is flimsy and often quite wrong, especially in the Humanities, where real experience, rather than scientific experiments, is all. For me, now, in this isolated canyon, experience was taking my mind away from abstract thought and forcing it to focus on aching muscles.

Back on the trail, I went around the first of Salt's two eastern side canyons, massive in their own right. The trail stayed away from the edge. I passed in and out of three gullies—little drainage ditches that I would not want to cross in a downpour—and then the trail cut back from the edge until it dropped down into another wash and moved closer to the edge, but never close enough to be called an exposure. As the trail turned the corner to the south, toward Salt, I stopped once again to get my bearings and let it all sink in.

At last, I had my "solo strategy" down pat, and although I now knew that I would be stopping at Salt and skipping Monument, I would pick up Monument on the return trip. Because I had shed the weight of several caches, the pain of the last couple of miles had not been bad, and I was almost to my second night's stop, a solo site. It occurred to me that the *less* the pain from challenging myself outwardly, the *more* I was ready for inward experience. The tragedy of our cultural bias is that it favors the outward journey at a terrible cost to the inner one. I had had to work through all of that; it had taken me three trips, but now I felt in my gut, as well as my heart, that I was finally at the point of something significant—here was the reason to do all this, even in my fifties. I was getting a feel for the "luscious solitude."

1. Slot Canyon Intrusion

Ah, love, let us be true
To one another! For the world, which seems
To lie before us like a land of dreams,
So various, so beautiful, so new,
Hath really neither joy, nor love, nor light,
Nor certitude, nor peace, nor help for pain;
And we are here as on a darkling plain
Swept with confused alarms of struggle and flight,
Where ignorant armies clash by night.

—*"Dover Beach," New Poems*, Matthew Arnold,
(Macmillan and Co., 1867)

I had arrived at the point where the trail began its descent into Salt Canyon. I was approaching the only real slot canyon from Horseshoe Mesa to Hermit, and there was a marvelous view. There is something about the narrowing of the walls of a canyon that increases the sense of drama and beauty. The stillness of the Tonto is incredible. There was a flat rock off the side of the trail, perfect for "pack setting." If I sat on the ground with my pack on, I found it all but impossible to get back up without rolling over and getting dirty. Alternatively, if I slipped out of the pack mid-trail, I struggled to re-harness. Thus, a rock with enough room to accommodate both me and my pack, preferably with the pack supported a little above my butt, was a thing to be celebrated. So much so that I took to writing in my trail notes where such "pack rocks" were to be found.

I checked the map and saw that the trail out of Salt Canyon beyond the Salt Creek crossover did not come close to the edge until the switchbacks at the very end, and from there they should be nothing to worry about—switchbacks always indicate safe passage if you stay on the trail. I reckoned I was comfortably within reach of Salt and would arrive with plenty of time for some afternoon "sightseeing," so I pulled out a pre-lunch snack and settled down for a decent rest.

Refreshed, I set off once more and soon came to a marble-colored slot rock canyon opening up before me. I slowed and walked carefully, for here the trail began a switchback and a steep descent toward its crossover with Salt Creek. I could see through the slot down into the Vishnu schist of the inner canyon but, as usual, I could not see the river. There was an obvious pool of water within the slot, probably left after the last rainfall and, as no direct sunlight could reach it thanks to the high walls of the canyon, it had not dried out. The slot was not very long, perhaps a couple of hundred feet or less. I was surprised that none of the guidebooks had mentioned the possibility of finding water here, but was also happy that I would now have water for my return without either carrying or caching a supply. It was a luxury not to have to worry about water.

I looked around and noticed a camping spot a short distance above the trail—a flat spot of cleared ground next to a large rock and some grass. I plopped my pack down against the rock and rolled my sleeping mat out on the grass.

Thanks to my cache system, I had made the trip without enormous strain. I had made it to Salt and was lying with my legs propped above my head on the edge of a big rock, holding the map over my head while checking out the miles I had just walked from the map's perspective. I had arrived by noon and could now enjoy the bright sunshine of the canyon all to myself, resting, eating, drinking, and reveling in an entire afternoon in which to exult in the panorama around me. I was beginning to understand. This canyon was to be enjoyed, not conquered—it obviously never could be conquered, but it could surely be missed if not in the right mind. Not many get this message; it is the intensity of the experience that counts, that dictates a solo strategy and the shortening of the daily walk, to leave time for reflection—not structured thinking, not "meditation," not trying to be profound, just letting one's mind do its own thing, without intrusion from others. This little plateau just above Salt's slot canyon was silent and comfortable, the grass on which

I lay acted as a bed of sorts, the sun was warming, and the slight breeze refreshing.

The map revealed why the almost 5 miles between Horn and Salt is one of the longest between-canyons trails in the park. Horn is very narrow compared to Salt, and its only camping spot is on the east wing of its two-pronged creek. When leaving this in the direction of Salt, the trail follows the west branch of Horn Creek and then does a little jog in and out of "No-Name Canyon" before swinging out to the edge of the Inner Gorge and the large ins and outs of the two very wide eastern side canyons of Salt. Finally, it heads south for some distance before reaching Salt and the creek bed.

As I took my rest next to the large boulder, thankful for the comfort of the tall green grass, I noted on the map that Dana Butte, 5,036ft at its peak and 4,206ft where it is closest to the Inner Gorge, has forced the Colorado River northward in a wide bend before it returns to its southwesterly flow. Dana Butte gives the Salt Canyon greater width than most of the side canyons and has created almost a dual canyon—Salt Creek has carved the west canyon and the runoff of the water from Dana has created an east canyon. The east side of Dana is quite steep and large boulders have rolled down it into Horn Creek, and thence to the Colorado, where they have accumulated to form the Horn Creek Rapids.

The region through which I would walk the next day is known colloquially as the Alligator, and, when studying the map in order to plan my itinerary, I could see why: the Alligator's open jaws are represented by a small canyon cut below Cedar Springs, while its back is formed by the eastern slope of Salt. What I had not previously noticed, however, was that, despite its somewhat whimsical name, the trail that followed the Alligator's right-hand snout suffered from a marked exposure. Of course, experienced trekkers would probably have no fear of such a drop-off—there are far worse ones all over the Grand Canyon—but to me it looked ominous, and I would rather suffer ridicule than death. Beyond the right-hand snout, the trail appeared to be easy, with no danger spots at all. I would take a second snack stop at Cedar Springs, which would, hopefully, offer shade and some water. The Alligator's lower jaw is a shortcut from Cedar Springs to Monument, with only two switchbacks into the Monument campsite. It is only 3.4 miles from Salt to Monument, almost 1.5 miles shorter than from Horn to Salt, so I should arrive in good time for my now standard leisurely afternoon, but I might even continue to Hermit, where there was reportedly a large swimming hole.

Plan made, I luxuriated in my surroundings. The afternoon breeze was bliss, my legs were recovering from the morning's exercise, and I took time to look around. To the northeast, but front and center in my view, was Hopi Point, and to its west, my right, was Mohave Point, looking down on me from the edges of what is called "The Hopi Wall," the large amphitheater that separates the two points. The next amphitheater over is "The Abyss." The walls between Hopi and Mohave were bright red. I was sitting in the middle of "The Inferno," which I could well imagine would live up to its reputation in July and August, but on this March day it offered the welcome warmth of spring.

After several hours of lying around, letting my mind do whatever it wanted to, I was ready to make use of the toilet. I clambered up the short path above the campsite and found a wooden toilet seat on a wooden box over a hole in the ground—no walls, no door, no roof. I imagined some old lady with binoculars catching sight of me from Hopi or Mojave and yelling, "Henry, come quick, there is a backpacker down there shitting in the middle of nowhere." To hell with them, I needed this toilet and was more than happy to enjoy its natural air-conditioning.

Dinner that night—at about 4:00 p.m.—was re-hydrated Lipton soup and veggies, all mixed together, with a side of crackers, peanut-butter, a handful of trail mix, and the standard-issue instant hot chocolate with marshmallow bits to wash it all down. Then it was time to fill the canteens.

The pool I had spotted in the slot canyon was perhaps 10ft long and 4ft or 5ft across. As I was drawing out water with the Guardian pump, something whizzed by just above my head. It was so fast and so quiet and so immediately invisible, that I wondered if I had imagined it. I continued pumping. But there it was again. And again. At last, I caught sight of it: a bat. Suddenly, I had the sense of being an intruder, like someone who would drive into lovers' lane with their bright lights on. Then, I thought about rabies, and what it would be like to become infected here, alone in this slot canyon in the middle of nowhere. I stopped pumping, moved quickly back from the pool, crawled flat along the rock, made it up onto a ledge, folded up the Guardian quicker than I ever had done before, and beat a hasty retreat to the campsite, still bathed in sunlight. I had one and three-quarters of a canteen filled. Obviously, it had been a mistake to visit the pool around the end of the day. After all, bats sleep until about four or five in the afternoon and when they wake, they are probably thirsty.

Now, I had a dilemma: Did I want to drink water, even filtered water, that bats had also been drinking? Then again, I argued, perhaps they weren't drinking it. Perhaps they get sufficient hydration from the bugs they eat. Perhaps they weren't protecting the watering hole but, rather, their nesting sites, along the edge of the slot. I didn't know. But I could imagine the headlines: "Man bitten by bat, suffers three agonizing days alone in canyon, dies next to pool of water." The rangers would read the story and shake their heads knowingly: "We warned him about going solo, but he had to do it!"

I dumped the water.

I stowed my fourth cache: "on way to toilet, go past standing yucca, then two yuccas on right—20ft more, black rock to left of acacia."

It had been a full day and I was ready for bed early, falling right to sleep in the soothing silence, only to be awakened a couple of hours later by the need to visit the wood-ring toilet. I made a mental note that too much salt in my diet was not a good thing. I had been drinking a lot of water but was also losing a lot through sweat evaporation, so a net excess of salt must have been playing havoc with my digestive system. I couldn't change my diet on this trip but would remember this for any future trips. In the meantime, I would drink even more water. After all, both Monument and Hermit had plenty of it. There is nothing like a desert to sharpen one's appreciation of water.

I snuggled back down in my sleeping bag and thought about the bats. I had no fear of them, but that feeling of being an intruder had unsettled me. It did seem like nature would rather get along without us, as it has for so many eons. I have always been skeptical of those who claim to "be one with nature." Maybe there are moments when that is so, but I think such people perhaps simply repress or hide the recognition that we humans are intruders. It isn't so much that we push nature around—like when we built the Glen Canyon Dam, flooded the Glen Canyon, and marked the cliffs of Lake Powell with a bathtub ring. Some of us, too many of us, do that. But surely, as bad as that is, it will happen for just a few more centuries at most and then nature will be rid of us.

The irony is that we are a product of nature and yet we are constantly at war with it, trying to use it, shape it, harness it, mold it to our needs and desires. But, if nature made us this way, is it our fault? For those who say that nature was made by God, I would ask: Could it be that myths should not be taken literally, that they are more profound when taken metaphorically and demythologized? God the "maker of heaven and earth," as the theologian, Langdon Gilkey (1919–2004), once argued with me, really means that the god/father archetype within us is creative, if we let that archetype do its thing. Much of mythology centers around the act of creation; if that is demythologized, then the creation is internal, an inner creation and not the beginning of the universe, solar system, or planet. Leave the latter to the scientists; let *us* focus on the inner journey.

True believers in religious myth need the literal meaning because they want to have a miracle upon death, to be given a life after death, an eternal life. I ask, is it not better to experience the eternal within this one life that we do have? Thoreau thought so: "Time is but the stream I go a-fishing in," he said. He had moments wherein time stopped, and he experienced the eternal life, standing outside of the stream/time. Any moving stream has the potential to evoke such ecstatic experience. To me, a god within seems better than a father archetype, hovering over us in the heavens like some all-seeing satellite.

Environmentalists love to blame those unlike themselves, those who do not love nature, for all our ills. But I wonder if this argument between them and the "anti-environmentalists" is akin to a lovers' quarrel. It seems that the environmentalists and their critics hate each other, but they both need each other: to love and appreciate nature, you must be able to live in civilization, for without that, you will have no comparison and thus no reason for appreciation. Furthermore, if this quandary between nature lovers and anti-environmentalists exists, then Matthew Arnold's poem "Dover Beach" was onto something: we live in illusion when we think life in nature is "a land of dreams, so various, so beautiful, so new." And when we are "being true to each other," then we must confront the truth that living in nature is also "here as on a darkling plain, swept with confused alarms of struggle and flight, where ignorant armies clash by night" (ibid).

I had memorized "Dover Beach," and other poems, after constant repetition, while walking the sidewalks of Hyde Park with a girl from the University of Chicago International House. I had always thought that the "ignorant armies" meant real armies, historical armies who are ignorant because they are not sure why they are fighting and are just obeying orders and others who make them fight out of some weird, psychopathic control obsession. Now, I wondered, was there another meaning that I had missed? Were Arnold's "ignorant armies" sides separated by an incommensurable experience, an abyss of different-ness, like men and women, like love and hate, like human nature and impersonal nature, like the intruder and the intruded? All such conflicts can lead to war, can they not? In *A Terrible Love of War* (Penguin Press, 2004), James Hillman put war into the context of love and illustrated his argument by referencing Arnold's "Dover Beach." He argued that "war [is] an apotropaic rite to keep death at bay by offering sacrificial victims," and he calls the body "death's instrument."

That night, alone in Salt Canyon, above the secluded pool, I fell asleep with questions of war swirling about my head and bats swirling about my tent.

2. Hermit Without Paper

I labour by singling light
Not for ambition or bread
Or the strut and trade of charms
On the ivory stages
But for the common wages
Of their most secret heart,
Not for the proud man apart
From the raging moon I write
On these spindrift pages
Nor for the towering dead
With their nightingales and psalms
But for the lovers, their arms
Round the griefs of the ages,
Who pay no praise or wages
Nor heed my craft or art.

—*"In My Craft or Sullen Art," The Poems of Dylan Tomas,*
Dylan Thomas (New Directions; Annotated Edition, 2017)

I slept late and left for Hermit Creek, via Monument Canyon, at 7:40 a.m. But despite my slow start, I still set off before the sun hit the trail and, as usual, prepared to have my breakfast on the trail after a little exercise. I walked in the shade out of Salt, stopped for my first snack, and then tackled the trail's first exposure. At the worst parts, just a foot or so from the drop-off, I practiced not crossing my legs but keeping the right foot, the one closest to the drop-off, always in front of me and my pole, then bringing the back foot up to my body. I focused on the trail, not the edge, breathed deeply, and moved slowly. Despite my fears, the exposure turned out to be not that bad, after all.

When I reached the snout of the Alligator, I found shade in another No-Name canyon and almost immediately was dropping down into Cedar Springs—no cedar, nor any other trees, no spring and, indeed, no sign that there had ever been a spring. I sat down on a rock, ate some trail mix, and moved on. On top of all its other shortcomings, Cedar Springs didn't even have a place to pitch a tent.

On the slope beyond Cedar Springs (now forever known to me as "The Devil's Misnamed Non-Springs"), I stopped to apply lotion to my feet. The sun was rising fast, and the day was getting warmer by the minute. I ate my breakfast of granola bar, power bar, and water beneath the Tower of Set rising more than 6,000ft above me.

At the top of the slope, looking down on Monument, I stopped again to take in the view and to check the map for distances. I had been caching supplies again and my carrying weight had dropped considerably; the daily hikes were becoming less arduous. For once, I thought, my planning was paying off.

Monument is the second largest of the four canyons in the Threshold section of the park, at least in terms of its number of campground sites. The trail drops steeply to find the stream bed just above the tower of rocks that gives the site its name. There is water here all year, and at the time of my visit the creek was running at much more than a trickle. A quick glance at the map explains the anomaly: the principal Monument Creek goes back all the way to the Abyss. Along its length, it is met by many side creeks so that, by the time it reaches the Monument crossing, it is a permanently flowing creek or even small river, depending on the time of year and the weather. Now it was a small creek, and quite delightful.

The campground was at the junction of trail and creek, but upon passing through it, all I saw were thick, low, acacia trees with thorns and no leaves. It did not look at all inviting. The spread of the low limbs meant that you could not walk from campsite to campsite without getting thorns in your face or having them catch on your backpack, and the sites were crowded together. Considering this was the only sizable campground between Indian Garden and Hermit, it was a disappointment. Pruning the acacia trees—something that happens naturally when there are animals to nibble them— would have made a big difference. No matter, I was now determined to go on to Hermit, so would not be staying, but it was good to be prepared. On my way back I would see if I could figure out an alternative to this official thorny site. I filled two quart bottles at the stream and went on my way.

On climbing out the west side of the campground, the trail passes the Clivus Multrums, with solar cells hooked up to power fans. From there it splits, one trail going left where a sign showed a tent profile and a "G." I had no idea what the "G" stood for, but it was a secluded site built into the cliff. It would be private, for sure, but far from the creek, too far to hear the soothing sounds of flowing water at night. With so little moving water in the canyon, to be away from the river seemed a waste.

The other trail followed the west side of the creek until it reached a sign indicating a side trail to Granite Rapids on the Colorado River. This is one of only two trails leading to the river—the other is Hermit Rapids Trail. I had been considering a day trip to the rapids on my return, but I didn't feel the pull of the Colorado for camping—the river means boat parties and you are always in danger of having to share your "solitude" with loud and excited visitors.

The trail to Hermit snakes up a west-side drainage. Like Horn, Monument has two drainages that meet at or above the trail crossing. The west drainage is very much like a side canyon and is sufficiently wet to have a wealth of vegetation, making for a pleasant climb up and around. Although I was anxious to get back on the Tonto Plateau, I lingered in West Monument. The trail took me a good deal south and, following the west side of Monument for a while, climbed steeply to a point overlooking the Colorado. There was little shade and the umbrella had been a lifesaver through the hot climb, but as I reached the viewing spot, it collapsed on me. I settled on to the pack bench, poured a quart of the Monument Creek water over my hot feet, dug into some trail mix, and then began the climb around another No-Name wash. It was already noon. Next was the junction with the Hermit Trail coming down from Cathedral Stairs and Cope Butte.

The descent into Hermit was longer than I had anticipated, with no afternoon shade and very few benches or pack rocks, but still I saw no one. Apparently, my fellow trekkers had not yet made it to Hermit Rest; but no doubt they would file into the campground later. Hopefully I would get there ahead of the crowd and would be able to pick a good camping spot.

After a couple of short switchbacks, the trail at last reached the Hermit creek-bed. I turned to the right and found a spot near the rim of the riverbank, where I would be able to hear the stream at night. There was a big boulder that would serve as a back support, some good flat rocks for cooking, and a nice spot for the tent under an acacia tree, not yet blooming but taller than those in Monument, and there was even some grass under it. In order of importance, my criteria for "the best" camping spot are: close to a creek for the sound of running water; far away from the bathrooms; some distance from other sites, preferably on the edge or somewhat separate from the majority of the sites; interesting topography, such as big rocks, a ledge, an interesting tree or other vegetation; and sufficient flat rocks to form the rudiments of a kitchen without setting the stove and pots on the ground.

I set up the tent, staking my claim to the spot, ate and rested and then went off to check out the plunge pool just the other side of the boulder and roughly 30ft below. It was a good size, bathed in sunlight and totally deserted. I stripped off down to my bare skin and dived in. The water was about 4ft deep, perhaps 6ft at its deepest, and I floated and dived to my heart's content. I must have stayed in that water for close to an hour and still no one came. The rocks were still bathed in sun when at last I got out and, as I was totally alone, I stretched myself out to air dry. Another hour passed until, at last, I began to get cold, so I dressed and used my hand towel to dry my hair. I was refreshed, clean (ish), and at peace. I walked back up the trail to check out the main Hermit Camp area. In years past it had been an established tent camp but was long abandoned and now is a campground like most others. On the far side of the campground, I found a cave site. It would be an interesting place to stay, isolated and far from the crowd, but I preferred the sounds of the creek and the proximity of the pool, and besides, it had been claimed by a party from Colorado State University.

I went back down to the creek to fill my canteens, making sure that I was not too close to the dunk pool and brought it back to my stove to boil. I only drink twice-treated water, either cleaning it with tablets or filter, or filter and boiling. John Annerino warns against drinking the water in Hermit Creek and Indian Garden Creek—the latter because it is polluted by mules, the former possibly because of the number of people that use the plunge pool.

As the sun dipped behind the west rim of Hermit Gorge, I fired up the stove and boiled some of the water in the little coffee pot. Next, I washed the dishes that I had used at Salt and made some hot chocolate, soaked the rice soup in the pot, reconstituted the dry milk and mixed the pudding, heated the soup, and sat down to eat: crackers, soup, pudding, hot chocolate, and cereal. Finally, I boiled more water for tomorrow's canteen.

Later, as the sun was setting, I was invited over to visit with the Colorado State University kids in the cave spot. I realized, not for the first time, that when hiking alone, I seemed to attract company. Perhaps people thought there was something wrong with me and that they could help. Sure enough, no sooner had I arrived at the cave site, than I was asked if I needed anything. Well, I was certainly low on toilet paper. No problem! A roll was immediately found and handed over. I was delighted... grass is no substitute for toilet paper.

The students were curious about my itinerary. I told them I was going back to Monument tomorrow. Then the next day to Salt, and then to Horn, and finally, because I never again wanted to sleep at Indian Garden, I would go from Horn to the Bright Angel Trail and the rim in one day. I would use the water at Indian Garden, but I wouldn't stay. I added that I would work on fixing my broken umbrella at Monument since I would have all afternoon there. In turn, they told me they were staying two nights at Hermit and one at Monument before going back up the Hermit trail. It meant that I would be gone from Monument before they arrived. I greeted this news with equanimity—I had enjoyed their company, was grateful for the toilet paper, but was already looking forward to regaining my solitude.

I slept very well that night, and at first light was packed up and on my way. I would breakfast at Monument, 2.5 miles to the east, and thereafter hoped to find an alternative to the Monument campground with its low-hanging acacias. Or perhaps, if I arrived early enough, I would find a secret spot away from the thorny bushes and the other campers.

3. The Ecstasy of Monument Creek: Panology

I passed no one on my way back to Monument, but when I arrived, it was to find the campground occupied by male students and an administrator from the University of Texas. They had filled the two big sites just upstream from the trail crossing. Downstream, the sites were lousy and, thanks to the acacias, there was barely room for a tent anywhere in the main campground. All that remained were the sites away from the stream and close to the toilet area, and those were singularly uninviting. Besides, I had to prepare water for my trip back to Salt, so wanted to be close to the stream. Reluctantly, I accepted that I would have to take one of the acacia sites.

The Texas boys were leaving the next day and I was prepared for a noisy night of loud conversation and laughter, but no matter. I set off to the Multrum toilets in the heat of the afternoon and then, about 40ft upstream, I noticed a faint path leading off the Tonto trail. It snaked off towards the ridge that overlooked the canyon. My curiosity piqued, I followed it down the hill and arrived at a sandy spot just large enough for one small tent between two rather flat boulders, next to, and about 10ft from the stream. It was at the base of a cliff, a towering pinnacle of rock that climbed up about 500ft and was topped by vast boulders that sat precariously near its edge. The creek was running right in front of me and was clear and perfect for filtering; the stones and boulders were ideal for sitting and cooking on; the ground of the tent site was soft sand, maybe dug out of the stream over years and then bleached white by sunlight. Beside the two flat rocks were two beautiful yucca bushes, as if some landscape designer had created the place. I looked up- and downstream and saw no other sites—I would have complete solitude.

Fearful of losing such prime real estate, I rushed back to my belongings and then ran back down the path. The site was still empty. I raised the tent and settled on to the flat rock. The toilets were neither in sight nor earshot and there was a small plunge pool about 30ft downstream from me. I could hardly believe my luck. I had never seen such a campsite below the rim and in the Corridor and was prepared to guard it jealously. I opened my pack and rolled out my sleeping bag onto the rock next to the tent site. I spread out, making it clear that the entire site was occupied, and offered silent thanks to Tyche, Goddess of Luck.

I had the rest of the morning and the entire afternoon to soak up the beauty around me. I decided to give up the trail down to the rapids; instead, I would lie on this large boulder and simply take in the world above and around me. Between the site and the stream there were some willows, but they were sufficiently downstream that they did not impede my view of the water; they simply enhanced my feeling of solitude and privacy. I strolled down to the creek's edge and dipped my feet into the stream to cool. Then I ambled down to the dunk pool. It was much smaller than the one at

Hermit and siltier, but it would still be refreshing. Its sandy bottom was stirred up by the small waterfall that filled the basin. I lowered myself in and stood still to allow the silt to settle before splashing water all over myself. There were birds all around—apparently, they also knew the spot was special.

Some high clouds were moving in, but they were unthreatening. I returned to the tent site, boiled and filtered my water for the next day, ate some lunch, and then laid back on the flat rock to enjoy the afternoon sun. I napped; the sound of the creek lulled me into sleep. I felt good.

My thoughts drifted home to New England, to my wife and our two children. I would love to show them this place. Perhaps one day we could all come together.

A couple came down the trail for a dip in the pool, but seeing me, turned around. Perhaps they sensed that I wanted my solitude. I was glad. Solitude was making this trip like none of the others.

Shortly after they left, I heard a strange sound, something like a grouse; once and then, a minute or so later, once again. My curiosity was roused, but I was too lazy, too languid, too enveloped in my "stone time" to investigate. I let it go. But the repeating of the sound continued and grew throughout the afternoon, becoming louder and more frequent as the long shadows heralded the approach of early evening. I could not figure it out, and yet, still it came, echoing off the stone cliff that towered above me. I had so long been in silence, this new noise was enchanting.

And then, at last, it clicked—frogs. Frogs in and around the stream, their calls bouncing off the cliff walls and magnifying in the echo. Soon I was surrounded by an incredible symphony of "walla, walla, walla." Night was falling, the clouds had dissipated, and a new moon rose in the sky. It was warm and breezy. Bats zipped through the canyon space, and the jagged edge of the monolith above me sliced into the surprisingly still-bright sky. And still the frogs sang.

A large ram appeared near the top of the cliff. I stared at it. I had read that mountain sheep were seldom seen anywhere in the canyon. Yet, unmistakably, there it was: not a short horned one, but a large ram, with curled horns, standing motionless and proud in the last of the day's sun. In my trail notes I named the spot Walla-Walla Waldorf. The deer at Indian Garden, the Texas Longhorns at the acacia patch, the frogs, the birds, the mountain ram—there was wildlife galore! And here was I with a front row seat.

It seemed that the rain was going to hold off for at least another day, but I attached the tent-fly just in case. I was sad that I could only stay one night in this magical place and took to my notebook to summarize the trip thus far: "Archetypal Trip: to Horn Creek by the Bright Angel Trail and Tonto West trail to Salt, dodging its bats, then to Hermit for my first social encounter, then to Monument, allowing a very early arrival in order to get to the Waldorf. Frogs, Ram, Moon, Echo." It is the longest single entry in that year's trail notes. For most of my life I have had the habit of recording extraordinary events—emotions, visions, dreams, notions. (I studied dream analysis with a Jungian, June Singer [1920–2004], as part of my Ph.D., making notes of all my dreams as soon as I awoke, and then discussing them with her later by appointment. She published one of my dreams, a "big" one, in her book, *Boundaries of the Soul*, Anchor, 1994.) It seemed that this extraordinary canyon was encroaching on my soul.

As the evening set in, the clamor of the frogs grew. My mind was on "wild," racing hither and thither. I took a sip of whisky from my little airplane bottle. I have always enjoyed a drink when I am happy, when my soul has been evoked or moved, so to speak. This seemed the perfect moment.

As was my custom, my mind did whatever it wanted to do, so it went back to the sight of that long-horned ram. Could I have been mistaken? Possibly—it had been a long way up and I could no longer see it anywhere. Perhaps it had been a hallucination. I had never before had a hallucination, but who knew?

Years later, when I was reviewing my notes for this book and came across the page describing my stay at Monument Creek, I found that, after the description of the site, I had written three words, capitalized on the first letter of each word: "Grand Canyon Panology." I was startled. It was the first time I had coined the word "panology." I had been using it in my teaching ever since that solo hike, but had forgotten that that was the moment at which I invented it. I did remember the deep-nature-absorption experience and ecstasy, since they are literally unforgettable, but not that word. And yet, that one word would become the goal of my entire intellectual inner journey. "**Panology**": the synthesis of demythological religion and anti-positivistic science—the logos of the whole, of "Pan."

I have always known that religion and science were incommensurables. Some years ago, but after my Grand Canyon trips, I created the acronym TIE, "The Incommensurable Experience"—the realization that we humans have mind-in body plus what the primitives called "spirits," the Medieval Christians called "soul," and Plato and I call "psyche." The subtitle of this book, "The Psyche of Water and Stone," comes from remembering that early evening ecstasy, while I was lying on "Pan's Rock," listening to the water and its frogs.

As I write, some thirty years later, it seems to me that on *that* evening in *that* place, I was given the notion that somehow the two incommensurables—religion and science—can be reconciled, can be merged in a "panological synthesis." Perhaps that is what Thoreau was thinking when he wrote in *Walden*:

> If you stand right fronting and face to face to a fact, you will see the sun glimmer on both its surfaces, as if it were a cimeter, and feel its sweet edge divining you through the heart and marrow, and so you will happily conclude your mortal career. Be it life or death, we crave only reality.

> —*Walden*, Henry David Thoreau (Ticknor and Fields, 1854)

A fact with two surfaces, as described by Thoreau, is a mixed metaphor applicable to an object or piece of nature. According to Mircea Eliade, primitive cultures can experience any object in two ways: as a simple object of nature and as a "hierophany revealing the sacred and therefore having an altogether different significance." To use Thoreau's other metaphor, the cutting of the blade, "dividing you through the heart and marrow," we carve out a meaning from the unconscious. Thoreau used the word "fronting" as a verb, meaning to look at or confront something, or someone, that can be seen in two ways, according to appearance and "inner reading."

Carl Jung also tried to create the coincidence of opposites, the coming together of the inner life and the exterior life by what he called "synchronicity." Thoreau once looked at his hand, and counted off his five fingers, comparing them with the peaks of the White Mountains in New Hampshire, and thus arriving at an incommensurable experience. Both finger and mountain peak are material objects. However, one of them is ours—fingers that move when we will them to do so— whereas the other, the mountain peak, clearly does not respond to our will. Since Thoreau explored the White Mountains, he saw them as something integral to him. Any fronting of an object can lead to usefulness or the perception of beauty, or its opposite. Alternatively, it can produce an image that enters the heart emotionally and evokes one's common unconscious to deliver a new thought or idea.

Now, as I write, I do so from a position of knowing a good deal about Pan. I have studied James Hillman's *Pan and the Nightmare* (Spring Publications, 1972) at length. But then, on that night at Monument back in 1993, I knew little or nothing of Pan. I didn't know that he had an escort, a nymph by the name of Echo, nor that his sign was a ram, nor that he learned to play water reeds to make music. But even though I knew nothing of Pan, save that he was the God of Nature, and that Christianity had incorporated him into its image of the Devil, I had somehow, unconsciously for sure, put the reeds, the frogs, the echoes, the mountain ram, and the campsite, which seemed like Pan's grotto, together in my mind and come up with "panology."

The day after the night of the frogs, on my way back to Salt, I wrote "panology goes beyond depth psychology and archetypal psychology." My incipient "panology," was later reinforced by Hillman's book on Pan, and I realized that the depth psychology work of Jung and Hillman represented the only true intellectual efforts to fully demythologize Ancient Greek polytheism.

Looking back on that extraordinary evening it seems to have been an uncanny experience correlating so much with my notion of panology, a philosophy of nature. Jung defined it as "An Acausal Connecting Principle," a title he gave to one of his essays in *The Structure and Dynamics of the Psyche* (Vol.8, Collected Works, Princeton University Press, 1968). What is being connected is an actual event with a high degree of meaningfulness. In his Foreword, Jung reveals that in his experience the phenomena of synchronicity "have multiplied themselves over decades." They have also done so for me.

For me, panology embraces coincidence and luck as essential for psychic balance with an extreme intellectual education. It is the psyche, that which is deep and unconscious to the ego, that does the connecting. So, perhaps the notion that Monument "gave me" panology is not so unbelievable; surely, the "big" dreams I have had are uncanny but also the products of the unconscious when my consciousness was asleep.

When describing his own experience of ecstasy, Colin Fletcher wrote that he "had moved closer to the pulse of life." Also reflecting on his own philosophy, Plato said that "it is brought to birth in the soul suddenly, as light is given off by a leaping flame, and it maintains itself thereafter." And Nietzsche had a similar experience at Lake Silvaplana, writing of it in *Thus Spake Zarathustra*: "But then life was dearer to me than all my wisdom ever was."

From the distance of decades, I am sure that my experience at Monument produced another instance of deep-nature-absorption experience. In my memory of that evening, I moved into sheer bliss, an experience that I can clearly recall after almost thirty years. Indeed, that deep-nature-absorption experience is as clear to me today as if it had happened yesterday. This is what Plato referred to as "anamnesis"—the experience is so strong that its recall is easy, for, as Plato said, "it maintains itself thereafter."

As I recall the experience, first there was the feeling of ecstasy. The dictionary gives the synonyms of rapture, trance, and transport, where "rapture implies intense bliss or beatitude," transport applies "to any powerful emotion that lifts one out of oneself," and trance involves "a mystic or prophetic state of mind." The "self" means the ordinary person's mind and identity, thus, to be standing outside of it must be an *extra*ordinary experience—a serious confrontation with the collective unconscious, that which we have in common but know little about. The unconscious is "in" our mind but from the standpoint of the ego is outside of our consciousness. If that is so, then we are *all* capable of having such an experience. Modern psychology ignores all of this at its own risk. I am certain that having confrontation with one's collective unconscious is what makes our minds deep and comprehensive rather than shallow and narrow.

I started using the word "panology" in my classes without remembering where it came from, and as time went by, I researched Pan and put my findings in context with what I had experienced at Monument. But at the time, as I lay on that rock, in ecstasy, I knew nothing but the oceanic feeling of merging into all around me. For that one evening, at least, *I was Grand Canyon.*

I believe that all true deep-nature-absorption experiences have three things in common: first, they happen when one is alone, often after having been alone for several days; second, their intensity is quite high, meaning that they are both easily recalled after long periods of time and that at their core they have the experience of ecstasy; third, the ecstatic feeling gives one the conviction of being one with, or merged with, all around one, the "oceanic feeling" that Fletcher experienced in his solo hike through the Grand Canyon National Park. The phrase was first used by Romain Rolland (1866–1944) in 1927 in a letter to Sigmund Freud, and Freud himself used the term in several of his books of that same period. The unconscious is the source of such ecstatic experience, either if it recalls one's early childhood experiences (Freud) or if it recalls the "primitive" period of human history, when the unconscious spoke in terms of spirits, ghosts, daemons, or gods (Jung).

These characteristics distinguish the deep-nature-absorption experience from the very pleasant experiences of life that are more common, such as having sex, falling in love, having the joy of achieving something, winning something, having children, etc. Deep-nature-absorption experiences do not deplore or diminish the significance of these other "good" or "joyful" experiences, but they do seem to be on another dimension. The deep-nature absorption comes suddenly and forcefully, as well as joyfully. It is undoubtedly an inner experience, even if dependent upon the nature around one. It can be compared with a big dream, which can also be remembered over an enormous space of time. Both dreams and deep-nature absorptions strongly suggest to me that there is another dynamic going on within a person besides his common thoughts and feelings.

In summary, deep-nature absorptions give one the experience, almost, of "being someone else," of having two dimensions—one conscious, one unconscious, opposites that seek each other now and then, and in everyone's dreams. Ecstasy is a certain, intensive, transformative kind of joy. Plato considered philosophy to be something communicated secretively, person to person, a way of thinking that only a few can understand. It is my opinion that the resulting lack of empathy between the Platonic philosopher and most other philosophers is the absence of the deep-nature-absorption experience for those others. If true, then philosophy is isolated from ideological and speculative thinking, contrary to the public's view of it, and is a highly personal matter between like souls. (See James Rhodes, *Eros, Wisdom, and Silence: Plato's Erotic Dialogues* [University of Missouri Press, 2003].)

4. Nature Deficit Disorder

I have had no fewer than twelve deep-nature-absorption experiences, although they have differed in intensity. I have actively recalled them only recently, when I began the process of anamnesis, thinking back over my life some five years before the first writing of this book. As I have done so, I have concluded that a deep-nature absorption does not work a transformation by itself. Rather, the deep-nature absorption must be recalled and "worked" up in relation to life's stages and changes. Its significance is found only after much reflection. The dramatic nature of the deep-nature absorption and the ecstatic experience is necessary, for it demands that one pay attention to the inner journey more than focusing on the social environment. The fact that a deep-nature absorption is so often buried as something "strange" and dismissed by most medical scientists, does not change the fact that it is one of life's very "high points." Our modern secular world has yet to take seriously that the public, on the whole, suffers from "nature deficit disorder," which should include a deficit of both the inner journey as well as the natural world. It is why old people love to tell stories about their past experiences.

I was an introvert until my middle life, but the transformation caused by my deep-nature absorptions eventually changed me into an extrovert who loves to recount my experiences. This change made my latter years as a professor much more significant and joyful, as I got to know my students as fellow, learning adults. Indeed, in those latter years I would hold classes in the back room of a Boston bar. It was easier to talk of the mystical deep-nature-absorption experience and the literature relevant to it in a bar, while listening to jazz and (for those of us over twenty-one) sipping on a classic pale ale. Education should not be constrained in that which is conscious and ordinary. Philosophy can be the best subject, but often is as dry as autumn winds.

I have had no dramatic deep-nature absorption since my last one in 1994; my job now is apparently to assimilate those that I have had and to relish a feeling of gratitude towards them. I consider all of them rites of passage.

Some psychologists characterize deep-nature-absorption experiences as "dissimulation" as "to hide under a false appearance," and give them a negative, psychopathic meaning. Jung followed this path in *The Psychogenesis of Mental Disease* (Volumes 2, 3, 8 *Collected Works*, Princeton University Press, 1968). Freud also did so, considering dissimulation and/or "dissociation" in his essays on hysteria. Jung broke from Freud to deepen his esoteric knowledge and theological acumen and to construct his depth psychology. Fortunately, Jung's best follower, James Hillman, served as my last mentor at the University of Chicago, and indicated a major shift away from orthodox Jungianism by emphasizing soul (*anima*) above spirit (*pneuma*).

Jung constantly used a phrase he received from Pierre Janet (1859-1947) back in the 1890s: *abaissement du niveau mental* (the temporary overcoming of the ordinary mental consciousness by the unconscious, often called "dissociation" rather than disintegration). Freud was caught in the positivist impulse to call the psychology of the unconscious a "science." Jung split from Freud and wrote of his own "Confrontation with the Unconscious," a critical chapter in his *Memories, Dreams, Reflections* (Vintage Books, 1965). Here he published a recollection of his childhood as well as his dreams.

Sometimes a deep-nature absorption or "abaissement" is simply a lowering of attention, but at other times it involves "automatisms," the suspension of conscious mind to release subconscious images. It could be that the ram I "saw" on the top of that cliff, towering over Pan's Rock, was in fact an automatism. The point is that none of this is "abnormal" or a sign of disintegration or pathology, although it is extraordinary and something not commonly verbalized. I consider it a rite of passage into old age. It is science that whispers in our ear and urges us to ignore the evidence of unconscious intervention. What does it fear? Science produces technology, but it cannot satisfy our desire for ultimate concern, the elaboration of meaningfulness over superficial entertainment and wealth.

For Plato, the highest truths are *noesis*, "intellection," and *dianoia*, "thought," which involves "things," rather than "the intelligible." The inner journey is all about noesis and dianoia. Science and analytical philosophy practice *pistis*, trust, and *eikones*, imagination. Students are surprised by this. Surely, they argue, trust and imagination are subjective, like philosophy, while science applies to facts and is therefore objective. The philosopher does not need trust and imagination, because he lives with noesis. For example, I *know* that I had deep-nature-absorption experiences; I am not imagining them, nor do I have to seek or trust in the verification of another. Science deals with empirical facts, while philosophy deals in experiential facts, wisdom, and the love of truth. Scientists don't love truth; they love that which they cannot experience but for which they can collect facts. Science and the humanities are incommensurable realms of thought, and I would suggest that one explores both without engaging that which is objective or disparaging that which is subjective. Science is subjective—the scientific impulse is to go along with other scientists, to seek consensus. Philosophy, the love of wisdom, is objective, it deals with psyche, soul, it does not need experiments, surveys, or the *consensus gentium*.

Deep-nature absorption in early childhood is only recoverable when one passes the second stage of young adulthood, when one is becoming established and working on reorientation for the last stage of life. Recollection of one's past life involves looking for meaningfulness, for the highly intense experiences. The suppression of these, in both early childhood and young adulthood, is socially conditioned by our unsophisticated culture that does not understand that a meaningful life requires the rites of passage of the inner journey. Each one involves the emergence of one's collective unconscious, not only in deep-nature absorption but also in our dreams. My visionary experiences in the Grand Canyon created "the inner journey" for me, and I believe that all people can have similar experiences if they anticipate them and prepare for them. One cannot "make" nature ecstasy, but like the ancient shamans, one can follow a depth-psychological regimen, beginning with one's dreams and progressing on to "vision quests."

As children, we do not have the understanding and vocabulary necessary to recognize the meaningfulness of such experiences, and then, as adults, we learn to suppress them. The common mental disease of our modern (or post-modern) society is to think that the suppression of the unconscious is maturity and the key to a good character. Edward Abbey intuited this when he said, "only the half-mad are wholly alive." The so-called half mad are those who confront the unconscious and engage it in dialogue—the label "mad" is used facetiously by Abbey.

In his first book, *A Week on the Concord and Merrimack Rivers* (Princeton University Press, 2004), Thoreau claimed that "in my Pantheon, Pan still reigns in his pristine glory...". In his diary he wrote:

> Methinks my present experience is nothing; my past experience is all in all. I think that no experience which I have to-day comes up to, or is comparable with, the experiences of my boyhood. [...] Formerly, methought, nature developed as I developed, and grew up with me. *My life was ecstasy.* In youth, before I lost any of my senses, I can remember that I was all alive, and inhabited my body with inexpressible satisfaction; both its weariness and its refreshment were sweet to me. This earth was the most glorious musical instrument, and I was audience to it strains. To have such sweet impressions made on us, such ecstasies begotten of the breezes! I can remember how I was astonished. I said to myself—I said to others—there comes into my mind such an indescribable, infinite, all-absorbing, divine, heavenly pleasure, a sense of elevation and expansion, and I had nought to do with it. I perceive that I am dealt with by superior powers. [...] I wondered if a mortal had ever known what I knew. I looked in books for some recognition of a kindred experience, but, strange to say, I found none.

Indeed, I was slow to discover that other men had had this experience, for it had been possible to read books and to associate with men on other grounds. The maker of me was improving me. When I detected this interference I was profoundly moved. For years I marched as to a music in comparison with which the military music of the streets is noise and discord. I was daily intoxicated, and yet no man could call me intemperate. With all your science can you tell how it is, and whence it is, that light comes into the soul?

— *The Journal of Thoreau, Vol. 2*, Henry David Thoreau
(Peregrine Smith Books, 1984) [Italics are mine.]

When he penned this question, Thoreau was thirty-four years of age and had just eleven more years to live. Two years earlier, in *A Week on the Concord and Merrimack Rivers*, he had written:

Suddenly old Time winked at me,—Ah you know me, you rogue,—and news had come that IT was well. That ancient universe is in such capital health, I think undoubtedly it will never die. Heal yourselves, doctors; by God I live.

Then idle Time ran gadding by/And left me with Eternity alone;/I hear beyond the range of sound,/I see beyond the verge of sight,—I see, smell, taste, hear, feel, that everlasting Something to which we are allied, at once our maker, our abode, our destiny, our very Selves; the one historic truth, the most remarkable fact which can become the distinct and uninvited subject of our thought, the actual glory of the universe; the only fact which a human being cannot avoid recognizing, or in some way forget or dispense with.

Notice the "suddenness" of Thoreau's deep-nature absorption and the sense of a timeless experience interrupting the ordinary sense of the passage of time. I felt that way at Thousand Island Lake in my teens when, for about twenty minutes or so, I seemed to be in a timeless world of joy and ecstasy. The experience had been evoked by staring at the sunlight on the surface of the lake; the wind wrinkled the water's surface and made the sunlight dance continually. Several years later, at Minarets Mountain, I experienced a similar sensation when watching sunlight dance on a wide stream. Then the ecstasy lasted perhaps ten minutes. Both experiences (about eight years apart) seem akin to that of Plato's "leaping flame" described in his Seventh Letter. Plato insisted that such an experience of ecstasy was the foundation of his philosophy, something he could not explain to those who had never had such an experience. I follow with the same conclusion: deep-nature absorption is the root of my panological philosophy, focused on the soul.

Both Freud and Jung believed that the unconscious, unlike consciousness, is timeless. Thus leading to the conclusion that our only "after-life" is that of these suspensions of time in the deep-nature absorption's ecstasy experience, in this, our one and only life. To experience the eternal before death transforms death from a tragic event to something more like the end of a book. I do not see this as anti-religious; rather, it brings eternity into life on this earth. It reinterprets the religious belief of "going to heaven" after death and sees it instead as an experience of timeless ecstasy. If we believe that, then we can accept death as the end of ourselves, but not of our legacies. When we die, we leave behind those who love us, but we live on as memories within and from them.

Jung's book, *The Earth Has a Soul*, has a picture of the entrance to Jung's stone-built retreat at Bollingen, where the philosopher went to experience that archaic or original world just off the shore of Lake Zurich. The caption beneath the picture reads: "Our task is not to return to Nature in the manner of Rousseau, but to find the natural man again." The natural man, I submit, does not own a smart phone or create a "social platform." Nor does he spend most of his time polishing his persona, his mask.

The morning after my deep-nature absorption with the frogs, I packed up at first light, gazed once more at the now silent creek and the towering red limestone above me, and then turned away to leave this most beautiful *and* meaningful of places. I was on the trail shortly afterwards, arriving at Salt by noon. I had retrieved my caches along the way, and made use of the exclusive outdoor toilet.

Again, I lay down next to the big boulder on the grass and rested awhile, naked in the cool sunlight, before making my way on to Horn Creek, which was once again deserted.

The next day, all my caches back in my possession, I reached the rim and the end of my trip. I had done it. Unlike the excursions of the previous two years, it had been a success. I had achieved my goals and had even experienced a wholly unexpected deep-nature absorption. And yet, even as I made my weary way to the car and steeled myself for the re-entry into civilization, I already knew that I would be back next year, for one more solo hike.

The canyon and Pan had won; they had cast their spell and I was enthralled.

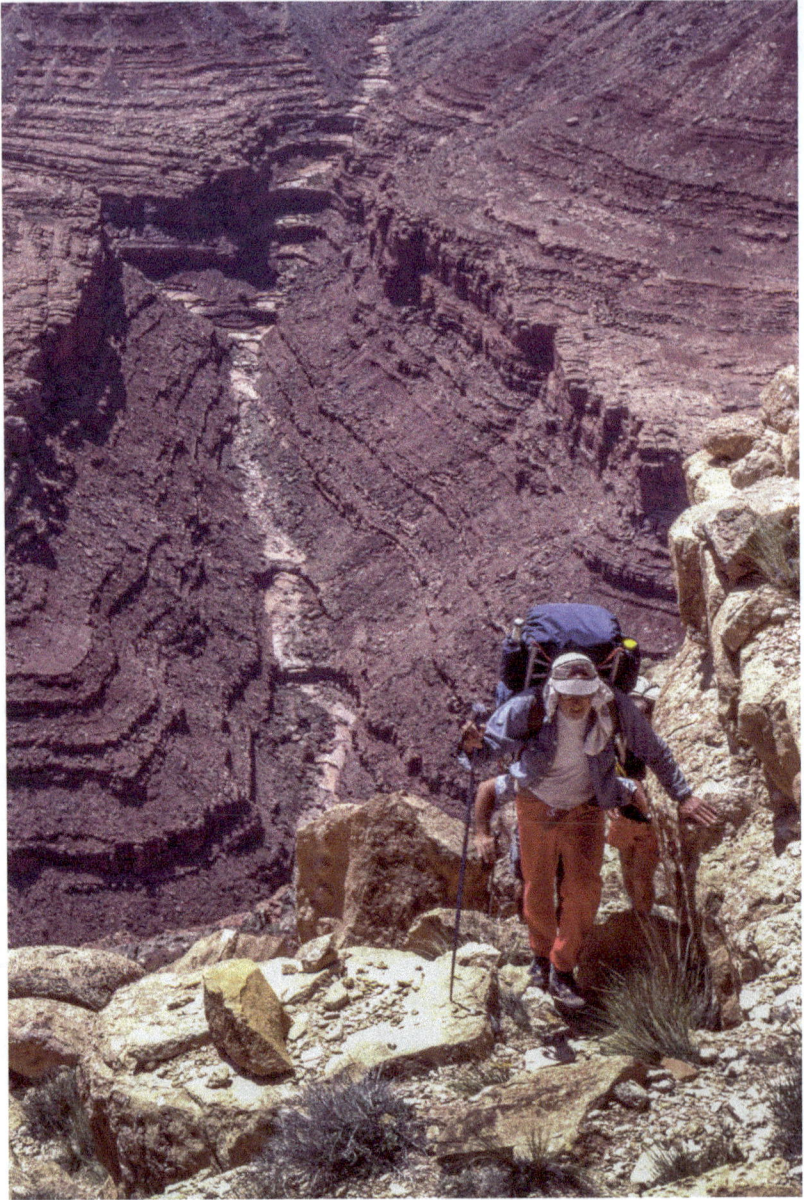

A backpacker climbing upwards towards the camera with a prominent V-shaped side canyon far below. *Photo by Gary Ladd*

CHAPTER 6

THE CANYON AND CULTURE

Side Canyons

· ·

1. Delight and Joy on the Trail

2. Death and Solo Hiking

3. The Sacred Canyon and Profane Users

4. The Native-American Vision Quest

5. The Inner and the Outer: Panology

As a child, I hiked many a trail in the High Sierras and all over the American West. I was a strong teenager, and I hiked with my father and brother. We took off from Tuolumne Meadows above the Yosemite Valley and hiked over passes and around peaks to the Merced River and down to the Nevada Falls and Vernal Falls. Later, we explored the Rae Lakes of Kings Canyon, where we were visited nightly by grizzly bears as we lay in our plastic tubes on the ground—this was before the widespread availability of light-weight tents and sleeping bags. Those early experiences taught me the "joy of the trail." I was young and strong, a high school athlete, and I already had a love of nature that seemed unquenchable.

1. Delight and Joy on the Trail

In my Grand Canyon solo hikes as an adult, I would meet almost no one for days, and when I did come across other hikers they would invariably be day hikers, or what I call "trekkers." Trekkers come to the Grand Canyon to conquer it, to set records and/or to obtain "bragging rights." Unlike them, I was there on "serious business," that of knowing myself, even though I was already in my early fifties.

What I found in the Grand Canyon was joyful, and my thoughts about those trips, partly revealed in my trail notes, were nothing less than "transformational." As I write this, I have a smile on my face, for in a way I am playing or dancing around a very serious matter. I am combining thinking with joyful experiences— *ecstatic* experiences—

that changed my life. I started my "Introduction" with a quote from Nietzsche. To me, those words speak of laughter and gaiety as well as contemplative thought. And what could be more laughable than to think I had ecstatic or mystical experiences after three days of solitude, lying on rocks, often next to creeks in various side canyons of the great Inner Canyon of the Colorado River?

In the Grand Canyon I let my mind run wild. I had no opposition because I was alone, blessedly alone, for several days. Nietzsche, I discovered, was right, there is such a thing as "joyful wisdom." So, dear readers, before castigating me for some opinion I may have expressed, make sure I am not playing with an idea or a thought. I enjoy puns, metaphors, facetiousness, and plain old picking up whatever thoughts come to mind and using them in one way or another. It is a way of thinking that I call *bricolage*—the art of using what comes to mind or hand.

Many people, perhaps most people, hike or walk to keep fit, to keep their physical body in good shape. But one can also walk for one's inner health, for the health of one's soul. Thoreau called this "sauntering." Every hike is a journey of sorts. One gets a good feeling from putting foot after foot onto the ground. A walking rhythm is therapeutic, and all walking (when there is an absence of danger or pain) is joyful. But one must *learn* to saunter, for sauntering requires the walker to have a "love of the ground," that piece of the globe underfoot that Thoreau called his version of "auriferous [golden] heaven."

2. Death and Solo Hiking

I have no prejudice against the tourist who comes to look at the Grand Canyon and wishes not to adventure below the rim. The rim itself is quite dangerous—many a tourist has plunged to his or her death simply because, for reasons they did not understand, they wanted to stand on the very edge of a 2,000ft or 3,000ft drop. Indeed, authors Michael Ghiglieri and Thomas Myers have compiled a book chronicling such deaths, on the rim as well as on the trails, in the side canyons, and on the river: *Over the Edge: Death in Grand Canyon*.

There is nothing wrong with wanting to experience the rim, nor with wanting to record the event in photographs. From the rim's edge at Mather Point (named for Stephen Mather (1867–1930), the first National Park Director, who started his job in 1914) there is an almost-sheer drop of 3,322ft to Pipe Springs, where the Tonto Trail crosses Pipe Creek. The sandstone monument at Mather Point hangs precariously over the rim as if at any moment it will break off and plunge its hundreds of viewers to their deaths. And, since one can drive to within perhaps 100ft or less of the Point's railings, access to this scary, dramatic site is incredibly easy, offering a cheap thrill that just begs to be captured on film.

Close to six million visitors come to Grand Canyon Village every year. There are mule rides and boat rides, lodging, restaurants, RV parking, a large general store, gift shops, paved roads, and even the city experience of circling in search of a parking spot. Park officials are amazed at how little time the public spends taking in the expanse of the Grand Canyon's vistas, and yet, ironically, there is so much else to do that the park administrators have, themselves, created and encouraged this disconnect.

There are, of course, many thousands who venture down from the rim. I have often hiked Bright Angel Trail in March, equipped with crampons, backpack, and two walking poles. I keep to the inside of the trail even at the top where it is 4 or 5ft wide, and I am invariably passed by an assortment of students on spring break. Almost always these young people are wearing sneakers, usually walking side by side, and sometimes even four abreast, with the outside person walking within a foot or less of the edge. At that time of year, the entire trail can be covered with ice and the "breaker" students are often slipping and sliding, which they take to be very funny, the boys laughing cavalierly, the girls giggling rather more nervously. Their absorption in themselves and their social relationships is astonishingly discontinuous with what they are doing: walking down a 20% slope, with a 2,000ft or 3,000ft drop just a few feet or even inches away from their feet as they pick their way down a treacherous icy trail. They are invincible, or so they think.

In 1993, it is recorded that seven deaths were caused by falls from the South Rim. In 2006, there were thirteen deaths, but it is not recorded how many were South Rim falls and how many were river or hiking fatalities. However, according to Ghiglieri and Myers, at least one person dies each year in each category. They write that "the lives were lost by sober, solid citizens who simply had no sense of danger standing on the rim of the mile-deep gorge. They died posing for pictures, leaning over for a better look, or strolling along rocky paths as nonchalantly as they walk through a shopping mall." After stating the obvious fact that warnings from rangers and signage "did not register," the authors reflect that "they were in a park, and that meant the authorities were responsible for their safety, weren't they?" Ghiglieri and Myers conclude by quoting Tom Jensen of the Grand Canyon Trust: "a lot of tourists approach Grand Canyon like a ride at Disneyland or some other amusement park, and think it's idiot-proof."

And so, armed only with our cameras, we continue to the edge across stones worn smooth by hundreds of millions of feet, focused merely on our need to "capture the moment."

On my first solo hike, I, too, carried a camera, but thereafter decided to see with my own eyes and to remember with my own brain. I do have two of my shots from that first trip displayed on my bookshelves, and I look at them occasionally. Conversely, I think of the Grand Canyon and remember the sights and sounds much more often, almost every good day. Some years ago, I stopped taking pictures altogether in the Grand Canyon National Park, and then at all other spectacular nature sites. Such a no-camera policy seems to enhance the vitality and precision of one's memory and experience of the "Wonder." Again, the Native Americans were right. To have one's picture taken robs the soul, not literally, but eventually and metaphorically, for a photograph may trigger a memory, but it diminishes one's ability to recollect deeply one's past, pulling all aspects of one's life into a whole.

The choice is philosophical: Do we pass our experiences through machines in order to authenticate them, or do we "front"—to use a Thoreauvian term—the thing itself in all its specificity, relying on our memory and experience when later we wish to recall the canyon? Do we return from the Grand Canyon to savor and learn from our memories, or simply to show off our photos to friends and family, implicitly saying "you really ought to go see it for yourself," and "I am way ahead of you; don't tell me you have never been?"

Since the 1960s, there has been an increasing cultural trend toward science, technology, and "cognitive studies" that ignore the psyche, i.e., any unconscious or mytho-poetic or imaginative dimension to life—hence, Jung's notion of modernity's lack of soul, which he explored in his 1933 book, *Modern Man in Search of a Soul.*

Beyond the photographs, though, how does one account for the common custom of throwing coins over the Mather Point railing? The National Park Service Rangers call the ledges beyond and below the railing "the zone of coins." But why does it happen? People throw coins over a railing apparently intending that they cascade down the cliff for "good luck." How is luck connected to such behavior? Wishing-wells collect coins because people like to evoke their wishes, often as a sideways communication to others in their party. But what is the connection between a quarter falling 3,000ft and one's luck? Is it some sort of sacrifice to whatever gods might lie below? Is the coin-thrower saying: "Here, death, take my token, but not me!"?

Latin baseball players often make the sign of the cross before stepping into the batter's box—an apotropaic device to ward off the evil of a 98 miles-per-hour fast-ball hitting their heads. The imaginary cross formed by fingers cutting the air in front of one's heart demonstrates to all—both the secular and the divine—that one's heart is with Jesus, and as Jesus's father is supposed to govern Fate, one can now face the coming baseball with no fear, and no doubt, raise one's batting average by fifty points!

3. The Sacred Canyon and Profane Users

Mircea Eliade used to say that "the sacred is anything that the human being experiences as extraordinary." That which is experienced in opposition to the extraordinary, all that is ordinary, is called "the profane" (see Eliade's *The Sacred and the Profane*, 1959). The term "unconscious" is often substituted with the term "subconscious," suggesting downwardness, just as the "unconscious" is often seen as a "basement" below the "higher" story of consciousness. This imagery is rooted in our religious pre-history, and the primitive (not "inferior") mind uses topographical symbols to express the idea. According to Eliade, "all religious sanctuaries or temples have three characteristics in the minds of the believers who construct them and originally worship within them":

(a) holy sites and sanctuaries are believed to be situated at the center of the world [what the Navajo and Hopis call the *sipapu*, said to be located a few miles up the Little Colorado River from its confluence with the Big Colorado in the Grand Canyon]; (b) temples are replicas of the cosmic mountain [as the Navajo consider Navajo Mountain and/ or the San Francisco peaks north of Flagstaff] and hence constitute the pre-eminent "link" between earth and heaven; and (c) the foundations of temples descend deep into the lower regions. [...] it was in Babylon that the connection between earth and the lower regions was made, for the city had been built on *bab apsi*, "the Gate of Apsu," *apsu* being the name for the waters of chaos before Creation. The same tradition is found among the Hebrews; the rock of the Temple in Jerusalem reached deep into the *tehom*, the Hebrew equivalent of apsu. [...] The apsu, the tehom, symbolize the chaos of waters, the preformal modality of cosmic matter, and, at the same time, the world of death, of all that precedes and follows life. ...The watery chaos that preceded Creation at the same time symbolizes the retrogression to the formless that follows on death, return to the larval modality of existence. From one point of view, the lower regions can be homologized to the unknown and desert regions that surround the inhabited territory; the underworld, over which our cosmos is firmly established, corresponds to the chaos that extends to its frontiers.

—*The Sacred and the Profane*, Mircea Eliade
(Harcourt, Brace & World, 1959) [Insertions are mine.]

The buttes and temples of the Grand Canyon, seen in the distance by the tourist, have been named after various gods: Buddha Cloister, Temples named after Deva, Zoroaster, Horus, Isis, Apollo, Brahma, Confucius, Diana, Juno, Jupiter, Manu, Osiris, Shiva, Thor, Venus, Vishnu, as well as the Tower of Set, Wotan's Throne, Cheops' Plateau and Pyramid, and Krishna's Shrine, to name the well-known ones. Temples are homologous to mountains here (point "b" in Eliade's passage above). Perhaps, those who believe that Jesus is the only holy god/man will be offended by the absence of Jesus, Moses, and the three patristic writers, Matthew, Mark, and Luke. (John, the fourth gospel "writer," was highly Gnostic rather than Christian [Elaine Pagels, *The Gnostic Paul* {1975}], but nonetheless is also omitted from the Grand Canyon.) There are reasons for the absence of Judaeo-Christianity in the park, but first and foremost I believe it is refreshing for the modern visitor to be reminded that there have been many other gods worshipped throughout history.

I have already suggested that imaginatively the Grand Canyon is the "center of the world," a psychic *sipapu* around which one is capable of reflecting on things on the grandest, cosmic scale (Eliade's point "a", above). The notion that one must be "in the center of the world," the *axis mundi*, is not egoism, but rather a psychic requirement: we have to wedge ourselves in to wherever we are and treat that "stand-point" as a center around which we orientate ourselves. That process of "centering" has been forgotten as modern people have lost their souls to technological accomplishments. We have created a cultural vacuum into which all intellectual sophistication is generally destroyed throughout Western culture. Religion loses any "objectivity" and is relegated to psychological need and fear, rather than being subject to reinterpretation.

Eliade's third notion (point "c" above) suggests the Grand Canyon's depths, where the Colorado River flows through the Inner Gorge, comprising nearly-two-billion-year-old rock. Like Eliade's "unknown and desert regions that surround the inhabited territory," these depths also homologize death. From the Tonto Plateau down, one finds a scorching desert, except in winter—I have found comfort in Cottonwood Campground on the North Kaibab, just below the North Rim, when the temperature at Phantom Ranch at the bottom of the canyon has been 120 degrees *in the shade.*

Thus, the tourist is confronting his own death as he looks "back and down" into time. When he tosses a coin into the depths, he is, perhaps, saluting the value, the *lucre,* of his life—a life that has always been an island or oasis surrounded by the waters or desert of death and formlessness. It does not matter if the Grand Canyon tourist does not consciously understand all of this. On the rim, there is little or no thought of death, but descend into the depths, and the potential for death is real.

The Anasazi Indians cremated the bodies of their dead on the lip of the Inner Gorge in the "primitive" section, just east of the Kaibab Trail, called "Cremation." I have stood there many times, indeed have spent a wondrous moonlit night there on "the Flats" beneath the towering, majestic Temple named after Friedrich Nietzsche's Persian namesake, Zoroaster (Zarathustra). My deep-nature-absorption experiences convinced me of the special nature of this place, and that it must be preserved by a wilderness designation. The rims can remain a designated "multi-use area," but the land within the Canyon should be a federally designated wilderness.

Obviously, the topography of the Grand Canyon envelops more than erosion and inorganic history. It is also, as pioneering backpacker and writer Colin Fletcher occasionally sensed, a psychic/alchemical laboratory concerning matter, death, and psyche.

Most of us may approach all of this hesitantly and tangentially, but approach it we do, in one way or another. The Grand Canyon draws one back, as if it holds unfinished business. For myself, whenever I return, it feels like home, even though I have lived on the shores of the Atlantic Ocean for fifty years.

4. The Native-American Vision Quest

The Grand Canyon offers an adventure on foot; this book has been an exploration, not an experiment, to find a qualitatively unique, or at least a very rare, experience not of adventure, entertainment, or physical feats, but of psychic discovery. My trips were similar to Native-American vision quests, although I "demythologize" those quests, believing them to be neither magical nor producing salvation; that is to say, they are not literally magical and do not produce salvation, they do not suggest an afterlife, and nor do they make one famous or unique. To demythologize is to interpret the literal myth by casting away literalism and transforming the myth to the logos of psychic meaning, what it says about the psyche. Metaphors replace magic; religious history is replaced by relevant psychology. Myths are not "false"; rather, they need to be de-coded. Myths are not about historical events, but rather, they are about psychic "events," i.e., experiences.

An easy example is the myth of Midas, whose magical touch turns everything to gold, thanks to a god's gift. Its meaning: Midas now cannot touch, kiss, or hug those he loves, a consequence he did not consider, but also—and more meaningful psychically—the lust for gold (money, wealth) results in alienation from those people we love or once loved, which is a price too high. Midas literalism is ridiculous, but the Midas psychic meaning is profound. The difference between the two? Demythologization.

I particularly do not like the word "quest," as if modern persons could convince themselves that they can quest and thereby "find" a vision by simply trying to do so. "Where there is a will, there is a way," is the idiotic notion of modern men and women who have yet to grow up. Equally I dislike the now somewhat popular notion of "soul making." In both cases, these notions depend on conscious, cognitive expression without any consideration of the depths of the psyche. The phrase "psychic depths" was given to us no less than 2,500 years ago by Heraclitus, who said, "If you travel every path, you will not find the limits of the Psyche; so *deep* is its Logos" (Fragment 45, my italics). Heraclitus's philosophy defies those who think psychology can be made into a science, "cognitive psychology." If *psyche has no limit*, then science, which measures things, presupposing limits to everything, cannot handle *psyche*. University professors are quite often careless of their presuppositions and subject to considerable delusions, since science is about the outer journey of career, wealth, status, leisure. Russian philosopher Nicholas Berdyaev (1874–1948) got it right: science is pragmatic, not ontological, regardless of its marvelous technology, whereas philosophical psychology is a matter of "ultimate concern" (see Paul Tillich, *Systematic Theology, Vol. 1* [University of Chicago Press, 1951]).

Psychic depths are what make living worth every moment, they bring joyful wisdom, which animates life. Perhaps that is one reason why my psyche was transformed when I descended into the depths of the Grand Canyon, seeking isolation and plenty of time to let my mind run "wild." That term is taken in Thoreau's sense when he said, "In *wildness* is the preservation of the world," referring to "inner wildness," not outer "wilderness." "Wild" certainly does not suggest misbehavior. Thoreau immersed himself in nature to bring out this wildness, not to advocate what today we call wilderness preservation. I am not against the latter but would emphasize the much more important "wildness." This is not a social or pathological wildness, the flaunting of laws and exhibits of narcissism, but rather it is the suppression of cognitive idealism and moralism, and the replacing of those "higher" matters with psychic depths, a primordial wildness. The human ego cannot control the psychic depths, regardless of its convictions. Thus, ultimately, the "depths" control the "heights."

All humans are capable of successful quests, but to achieve them one must first isolate oneself from others and from the habits of a technological world. In the Grand Canyon, one can easily move from one side canyon to the next by getting on the trail at first daylight and stopping at noon to set up the next camp site. The rest of the day can be spent looking around, lying on rocks next to streams, exploring. "Stone time" is necessary, but so, too, is "stream time," and going in the early spring or late fall allows one to spend time not only *collecting* necessary water but also becoming acquainted with water's own behavioral magic, meaning, and power. The Grand Canyon is, perhaps, the world's greatest exhibit of what water can do to stone over millennia of erosion.

This book is about how the physical world—perhaps best confronted in this one specific "desert in a large hole"—impinges on the psychical or "spiritual," and how the latter affects how we experience physical nature with our bodies. The deep-nature-absorption experience is the best example of the psyche acquainting itself with nature; its joyful meaning distinguishes it from illness.

Here the thoughts of the book closely follow the experience of the landscape. The origin of these writings was the discovery, while camping at Cremation, that the topography of the Tonto Plateau and the structure of the human mind are amazingly similar. The proper name for such a thing is "homology": the structure of two quite different things, even two incommensurables, are analogous. The obvious example of an incommensurable with which we live every day is the difference between mind or spirit and matter, especially that of our bodies. Scientifically, mind is a part of body; panologically, "body" has its own wisdom because it is connected to a primordial unconsciousness, and "mind" is psychic, not physical. The Grand Inquisitors believed that the soul weighed a certain amount, and any woman who weighed less than her height indicated she should, was burned to death. If a woman's weight was too low, it was clear evidence of an absence of soul and thus proof that she was a witch. My Dutch ancestors, in Oudewater, had a scale that deliberately over-measured a woman's weight so that she would weigh in above her designated "height/weight" and thus survive the Inquisition.

As you approach the Grand Canyon along Route 180, driving mile upon mile across the Colorado Plateau, it seems inconceivable that the landscape will dramatically change just a few miles ahead, even though the maps tell you that, indeed, this will happen. There are no smaller canyons, no anticipation of a sudden drop-off, just an endless vista of the same, rather monotonous, semi-barren landscape.

In the final approach, the upward slope ascends not to a mountain ridge or range, but to a huge, gaping hole that astonished the first Spaniards to discover it, and which had been a source of vision quests for the old Anasazi tribes long before the white man came. Here is a tangible example of a topological incommensurable, and the experience of one's first approach to the Grand Canyon is unforgettable.

Every day, most Americans must sludge through a wasteland of fast-food joints, boutique shops in endless malls of pseudo-wealth and oversized shoppers who appear to have no life beyond the next purchase. American culture now presents endless movies, books, museums, universities, and media events stripped of any depth or complexity, and we experience strip-malls, strip-joints, and often a stripped landscape that sells convenience, varieties of materialistic experience (with apologies to *Varieties of Religious Experience* [1902] by philosopher William James [1842–1910]), and superficial, often silly, spiritualistic compensations, which replace the needed consolations and enchantments that used to be central to human life. Yet, this "wasteland" can sometimes—at least for some—be followed unexpectedly by the intersection of the "extraordinary other." It could be the ten-year old boy playing stickball on the street, totally immersed in his imaginative world, or it could be the savage interruption of the Colorado Plateau. Seemingly out of nowhere, the landscape of experience drastically changes. As one pays one's fee at the Park entrance and, a mile or so beyond, pulls into the parking lot around the Canyon Visitor Information Plaza and then walks to Mather Point, one has a revelatory glimpse into another realm, wholly other than that of the Eliot-like wasteland seen upon approach. One walks down steps leading out to a column of rock that is almost ready to plunge into the depths.

The first time that I saw the Grand Canyon from this point as an adult, I experienced fear mixed with an incomprehensible astonishment. It was not at all clear what I was confronting, but what was very clear was the sense that the scene was "unreal." I had seen pictures, of course, so the reality before my eyes was vaguely what I expected. But the sweep of the views, the colors, the lines, the depths, the soft, almost velvety mantel, which is that of the Tonto Plateau. Here, decidedly, was the opposite of wasteland; here was *phenomenon,* a ghastly site, an event encased in a pronounced depth of time.

It has been the presupposition of this book that one cannot live without the knowledge that the future promises a possibly magnificent change in what it means to be human and to live on this planet. We live for metamorphoses, even though it is common to fear them as well as hope for them. Even if we are not bored—Dostoyevsky (1821–1881) rightly claimed boredom to be *the* modern problem—we look for significantly better experiences. We trudge on in expectation of a rush of psychic energy or creativity, of dramatic change—whether it comes from an experience of love, of ideas, of dreams, of a vision or revelation of some sort. We dream of "paradise," not of the past but of the future, and we always have. Apocalyptic visions, utopian hopes, the Western thesis of escaping civilization for an experience in the wilderness, expectant, youthful *puer aeternus* dreams, all of these are still at the heart of American experience. And yet, most who live near the East Coast have never walked down into the Grand Canyon, and many have not even visited the Grand Canyon's rims.

Somehow, when one first sees the Grand Canyon, the idea occurs that this is the best America has to offer: a country built around the dream of living close to nature, close to the extremes of wildness, silence, depth, beauty, and incomprehensible *expansiveness*. All of this is buried in the Anasazi vision quest; they intuited that if one isolates oneself in nature, something radical and good will happen. Sometimes the "thing" is death or derangement, but most often it is the turning of a page, from conventionality to the first steps into elderly wisdom, and eventually to the shamans, those who experience *The Wisdom of the Elders*—the title of a book by David Suzuki and Peter Knudtson, subtitled "Sacred Native Stories of Nature" (Bantam Books, 1992).

However, it is seldom understood that the shape of paradise, and the taste of its experience, might take the form of something we think we know so well, that of the wild and the "de-human." We want to shape paradise in our own image of ourselves. We imagine it as a sleepy place of "dreaming innocence," as Paul Tillich called it, for those who are not ready to live "after the fall."

Native Americans, like all archaic, shamanistic cultures, make the mountaintops of their landscape sacred places. Traditionally, sacredness comes from on high; mountaintops are inhospitable and seldom reached or "conquered," as we egotistically say. However, we need to demythologize the shamanistic experience and relate it, not to flying on high, but to descending into the depths of the human psyche. Visions are about the latter; those who do not have them will maintain the belief in magic and miracle, which will simply disappoint them.

Hell is in the depths, as in the lower levels of Hopi mythology, from which the Present People ascended through the *sipapu*, the hole from lower levels of Past Peoples to the present, higher earth (see Harold Courlander, *The Fourth World of the Hopis* [1971]). Paradise is not a place divorced from those who dream of it, but rather a paradox. Following the Adamic myth of Paradise, it is a place for which we long, but when we think we have found it, we humans proceed to mess it up. Two examples: Los Angeles in the 1950s and '60s had a number of massive freeways that allowed teenagers like me to drive at 80-90 miles per hour without risking a speeding ticket, since the roads were larger than demand required. It was a teenage paradise. Today, in the early twenty-first century, all five or six lanes in each direction have cars backed up and crawling along at 15-20 miles per hour. A paradox is a conclusion that contradicts a premise: the LA planners never imagined that their great highway, built for fast travel, would ultimately cause the opposite—massive traffic jams. If you overbuild, strangers will rush in, and underbuilding will result. Second example: The Grand Canyon covers an area of 1,904 square miles; the National Park administration excludes the public from about 1,800 of those square miles—despite the intention of Congress that the whole area should be designated a National Park. What is available to be seen and experienced is just 104 square miles. But, since people have been prevented from rushing in to experience all the Grand Canyon, the result will surely be the gradual development of the Southwest.

The Judaeo-Christian God tells us not to eat of the Tree of Knowledge of Good and Evil, suggesting that if only we dropped our *hubris* (pride), believing that we always know what and where good and evil are, then we would have paradise. Adam eats of that dangerous apple and sex then paradoxically becomes a problem rather than a delight, and we must toil to eat because we no longer have animal-like senses assuring a means in nature's naturalness. In search of wealth—upon which we project goodness, then make symbols (bills, gold, silver, mansions, precious anythings), until we turn wealth into power—we find ourselves with the predicament of Midas, unable to embrace others because all he touched turned to gold. American democracy is becoming an oligarchy of the rich and powerful. Alienation from nature seals our fate, for we have failed to realize that ancient myths survive for a reason. None of this receives appropriate, serious attention in our universities or high schools. Nor is this anything new: When thinking of the Harvard University of his day, Thoreau complained that it taught all the branches of learning but none of the roots. One of the roots is the danger of unlimited power and wealth; all roots go back to mythology seen psychically.

All of us seem to walk the flat-experienced earth with basements of evil and inaccessible elevations of sacredness. The moment at which we first look *down* into the Grand Canyon, we are met by a paradox: the paradox of a paradise below and, moreover, a paradise that looks *inhospitable, dehumanized, devoid of any welcoming oasis.* The amount of barren rock is overwhelming; the vegetation is sparse and spaced far apart. Even the cottonwoods of Phantom Ranch, tucked into the throat of Bright Angel Creek's delta, or Indian Garden, do not promise much relief from the vast slabs of vertical, barren rock and miles of rock debris that fan out below in every direction and at every different elevation for hundreds of miles. We wrestle with these two paradoxes—the inverted mountain and the apparent desert desiccation—for they make it interesting and enticing. Like all paradoxes, however, they are enigmas. The puzzle is solved only when such topography promises solitude and transformation if one is prepared and anticipating such. The Grand Canyon's beauty is not a paradise but, rather, it is a means to a vision quest and the experience of an inner journey and possible transformation. Here we have a "reversal of metaphors," the high being replaced by the low. The collective unconscious is low, threatening, ignored, until it offers ecstasy, suggesting that we have been looking the wrong way.

I suspect that callous tourists who casually call the Grand Canyon "the big hole" deliberately try to avoid the possible confrontation with psychic depths because they fear the change will suggest that there was something wrong with them. If approached without preconception, the Grand Canyon changes us. Usually, the fear of the place or the lack of fear wins out, another paradox. The South

Rim welcomes close to six million visitors a year, but only about 1,000 backpackers. Of that thousand, only a very few experience an inner journey along with a long hike.

Cremation, the at-large section just to the east of the South Kaibab Trail, is so vast that on any one night the number of backpackers on site could be multiplied ten times and still none would see another unless passing briefly on the Tonto Trail while leaving or arriving. Yet, above, at the rim, it is often a human "zoo."

There is a startling resemblance, a homology, between the topography of the Grand Canyon and the nature of our minds, and that is what is so mysterious and "grand" about the place. It teaches us a hard lesson about ourselves; it is a sort-of Socrates-in-stone. It so clearly suggests that paradise is approached by going down, not up, by descent rather than ascent, by exploring not the human but the "de-human," the uncivilized, the wild both in ourselves and in the canyon itself. Both the flatlanders and the ascenders—those who think they have a higher, spiritual nature, the Gnostics—are in opposition to such descent. It was even said once that Jesus descended to Hell to save the souls chained therein, but such *descensus* soon became heresy, and by the seventeenth century, the belief in Hell had declined, according to D.P. Walker (1914–1985), into therapeutic angst and metaphorical whimsy: "What the hell?"

Today people know too much, mostly trivial, while not knowing enough about how little they know. The proper term for their false certainty is "secular gnosis." Know-it-alls are, today, to be found everywhere in America; but they have no idea how large the "all" really is.

The experience of the Grand Canyon teaches you that some things are not accessible only through books, or even through culture as a whole. When you descend into the Grand Canyon, you walk back in time (as Colin Fletcher reminded us) and away from culture, away even from all those gods whose names are ironically attached to the pinnacles and plateaus within this largest cleft in the Colorado Plateau. Instead, you descend into one of the Grand

Canyon's most noticed mysteries—its abounding silence, a silence far beyond the mere absence of noise or talk, a silence that demands attention.

5. The Inner and the Outer: Panology

The other mystery here to be explored is the mystery of the Grand Canyon's age—not precisely its geological age, but rather, its *primitiveness*. Today the Grand Canyon is divided into Backcountry Zones: Corridor (fondly called "the sacrifice corridor"), Threshold, Primitive, and Wild. However, in the mind of Colin Fletcher, who walked through all these zones in his historic traverse from Havasu Canyon to Nankoweap, it all offers one united experience, which came to him several months after his "walk," as he was opening his poncho and got a whiff of Grand Canyon dust:

> I can find no adequate way to describe what my nose reported, for when it comes to smells our language is poverty-stricken. But I know that the instant I smelled the dust from that tattered poncho there surged back into my mind the reality of what life in the Canyon had been like. I do not mean just that I remembered specific details. I knew once more, in a flood tide of certainty that invaded all my senses, the forgotten essence—the whole clean, open, sunlit, primitive freedom of it.
>
> —Colin Fletcher: *The Man Who Walked Through Time*
> (New York, Vintage Books, 1967)

How can it be that trips that require close attention to the task of survival— when one false step can mean instant death or an agonizingly long experience of dying—give one a sense of "freedom"? How can freedom be "primitive"? Do we not experience more and more freedom as modern democracy and the advances of technology allow us to escape from the daily task of survival? Does not freedom exist in the present or future, not in the past? Do we not find freedom away from the dust of the ground, exposure to the elements, and freed from the solitude and monotony of wind, sun, snow, or rain always in one's face? Freedom cannot be found in ancient history, can it?

The freedoms afforded us by democracy and technology are entirely of the outer world. Wealth and power are the essence of freedom in the outer world, freedom to do what one wishes rather than be a "slave" to others or have a disappointing job. But the more important freedom is the freedom of the larger mind, the ego reduced by confrontation with the collective unconscious. No wonder Thoreau said: "In wildness is the preservation of the world." Real freedom comes from an inner journey born into our nature, into all of those who are human—a potential waiting for our egos to look away from our own aggrandizements.

This book, then, is ultimately about freedom, a strange kind of freedom, I venture to say, a freedom we once knew if, as children, we were fortunate enough to play in nature.

It is my belief that only about 15% of our cultural history is taught in our universities, with 85% ignored, because we think it is outdated and irrelevant. That 85% is everything before the "Enlightenment," before Descartes and Kant, before humans were "no longer anchored in Transcendence, have turned towards the sublunary [terrestrial] sphere, alterable by our own endeavors, so that we have faith in the possibility of earthly perfectionment" (Karl Jaspers, *Man in the Modern Age*, Doubleday, 1957). Indeed, the 85% is before the secularization process, the giving up of a transcendent "God" and the break away from the notion that history is in "his" hands.

There is a middle ground that takes in the study of the whole of knowledge, every relevant sphere of thought—psychology, philosophy, religion, literature, social ethics and cultural history, scientific methodology, political science, and the arts: "Panology." I have coined the word from "Pan" (the Greek god whose name means "all" or "all of nature") and *logos* (the Greek for "study" or "knowledge of"). Panology understands that modern man is fully engaged in dystopia—which he considers to be a utopia—but panology adheres to neither atheism nor a religious belief; it is, in no way, a "new age religion."

A simple way of saying this is that modern man is all mind, and pre-modern man was too little mind but also heart and soul. Panology seeks to balance all three in a unity, a wholeness. It starts by the synthesis of science and the "liberal arts" into a whole; a difficult task because each side scapegoats the other.

Colin Fletcher's trip from Havasu Canyon ended on what he called Beaver Sand Bar, where the Colorado river curves north and then south and east before turning west just beyond the Unkar Creek rapids, between the Cardenas Creek and the Escalante Creek. Fletcher was exploring the wildlife of that area, where he was camping, watching a rattlesnake, a toad, some mosquitoes, a dragonfly, and various sandflies, as well as a beaver. He describes what he called his "oceanic feeling," a term that was originated by Romain Rolland, from his study of Indian mysticism. Fletcher called it the "feeling of the eternal," and compared it with the ocean that once seemed to have no limit. Here, Fletcher is talking as a panologist:

> ...I no longer seemed to need examples. I no longer needed to concentrate on a deer mouse or a rattlesnake or a sandfly. For I was no longer a stranger in the deep and ancient world of Beaver Sand Bar. And I could move about almost freely, it seemed, through those long, quiet corridors of time that angle up and away from the first simple fragments of animate life. I do not mean that I gained any new intellectual insights. [...] Nothing at all that would help me to understand more clearly, in any intellectual sense, how all the scattered and disparate strands of life weave together, interlocking. But I had moved closer to the pulse of life. I had heard a new counterpoint to the unique basic rhythm of the universe. And in it I recognized the common grain that ran through everything I knew existed, including me. [...] Now [...] the sense of union had become explicit, intimate, totally involving. It embraced everything. Not only man and beaver and mouse, lizard and rattlesnake and toad, sandfly and slug. Not only thicket and willow tree. Not only the sand bar. But the rock as well. [...] And with the rock and the plants and the animals, even with the wind and its cloud

shadows, I felt, now, a sense of common origin and direction. *A sense of union so vibrant that when I looked back afterward I sometimes felt that the whole experience on Beaver Sand Bar was like a perfect act of physical love.* For the union was total and natural and selfish and unselfish, and beautiful and holy, and at the same time riotously good fun. And while it lasted nothing else mattered, nothing else existed.

—*The Man Who Walked Through Time*, Colin Fletcher
(Alfred A. Knopf, 1967) [Italics are mine.]

Thoreau wanted to "write nature," rather than to write about nature. He wanted a book that resembled the outside, to be comfortably and appropriately read out-of-doors, he did not want to write a book to be shelved in a library. More than 700 copies of *A Week on the Concord and Merrimack Rivers* were returned to him, unsold. His contemporaries were not ready for a book written about "the nature within" *and* "the culture without," rather than, exclusively, about natural details, as could be found in his journals after 1851. Today, original editions of Thoreau's book sell for well over $40,000 apiece and I submit that his modern popularity is because he dared to intertwine his views on culture, nature, and advancing technology. As I always told my students, it is better to mix the "bush" (nature) with the "box" (the office, the den, the writer's desk), in a wonderful balance of the two.

Those who write about the history of environmentalism—such as Max Oelschlaeger (1943–), a professor of philosophy whose *The Idea of Wilderness* (1991) reaches "from prehistory to the age of ecology"—talk about John Muir, Aldo Leopold (1887-1948), and Thoreau, "the Nature Trilogy." Oelschlaeger adds to this trilogy Robinson Jeffers (1887–1962) and Gary Snyder (1930–), two poets of the modern environmental movement. But other than these, writers of "wilderness philosophy" are typically professors writing about others who are writing *about* nature more than their personal experience of nature as it relates to the quality of life from a broad cultural perspective, requiring philosophy, psychology, and religion along with the history of science.

The other best-known survey is Roderick Frazier Nash's *Wilderness and the American Mind* (4th edition, 1982). Nash (1939–) looks at the work of the trilogy and adds the writings of David Forman (environmentalist agitator, 1947–), Bob Marshall (wilderness activist and scientist, 1901–1939), Marjorie Hope Nicholson (literary scholar, 1894–1981), Jack Turner (nature writer, 1942–), Edward Wilson (biologist, 1929–2021), and Donald Worster (environmentalist historian, 1941–). Yet, none of these later additions touch on the deeper disciplines of the "The Big Four": philosophy, the history of religion, comparative mythology, and depth psychology.

After Thoreau, the next panologist is Friedrich Nietzsche whose transformative experience, the vision of the eternal return, took place on the lakeside just north of Sils Maria, Switzerland. His apparent ecstatic experience hit him "out of the blue," evoked by the waterfall behind him and the beautiful lake in front of him as he was sitting on the sand with his back resting on a large triangular rock.

I live in the American East, beside the Atlantic Ocean, facing Europe, and yet I think of myself as a man of the West, as did Thoreau. He used "the West" or just "West" as a metaphor for his inner wildness; he always liked to walk "West" (not lower-case west) when deciding on a walk. Metaphor, symbol, and myth are always products of the inner journey; data, signs, experiments, and surveys abide in the outer journey. Dichotomies have their time and place, and are, like children's toys, aides in the process of growing up, becoming memorable relics once we have matured. Culture is a product of human development, but the lesson of this book is that culture cannot advance *further* without the advancement of human inner development. It needs panology—i.e., balance.

Just as I have sought the middle road between opposites in my thinking and living, I stuck mostly to the Grand Canyon's middle ground—that of the Tonto Plateau, 2,000ft or so above the Colorado River and below the South Rim. I camped only in "the Corridor"—on the Tonto Plateau between Hermit Creek to the

West and Horseshoe Mesa to the East. And, although I had three experiences of risking my life—two of which brought me close to dying—this story is not about adventurous hiking, and dangerous obstacles overcome. Most of the adventure was found in my "inner journey," *because* I chose to walk alone, in six trips, carrying everything needed to survive on my back. I do not deny that it was quite a feat, but the real feat was turning my Grand Canyon forays into an inner journey.

Colin Fletcher said of solitude:

> You cannot walk alone through virgin desert, day after day, without responding to the solitude. You do not grow lonely; you pass over instead into an aloneness that leaves you free and content.

I agree. Solitude intensifies one's experience and often springs open the inner life's need for the extraordinary. It was solitude that I sought and found in the Grand Canyon; it was spontaneous ecstasy that found me!

CONCLUSION

We are beset by an all-too-human fear that consciousness—our Promethean conquest—may in the end not be able to serve us as well as nature.

—Carl Jung, *Collected Works*, Volume 8
(Princeton University Press, 1968).

Solo backpacking involves living in a completely different way from that of most modern Americans: sleeping in a tent, cooking on a stove as small as one's hand, having a kitchen of one pot, one cup, and a small bag of food, much of it dehydrated. No ice cubes, no electronic devices—but also no one to tell you what to do, to say outlandish things and expect you to confirm them, no arguments except with yourself, total solitude for a week or so. I know it is the solitude and the preparations necessary to do such backpacking that are the major stumbling blocks for most of us to overcome. But consider the advantages in doing so. This book illustrates what preparations are necessary: not by preaching, I hope, but instead by illustrating what happens when you are *not* prepared.

But why would anyone venture alone into the Grand Canyon? Yes, it is a beautiful place, but there is an infinite number of beautiful places on this planet. In 1931, Carl Jung wrote an essay, "Archaic Man," in which he referred to the anthropologist Lucien Levy-Bruhl's study of "Primitive Mentality." Jung made what many consider an unbelievable statement: "...it is not only primitive man whose psychology is archaic. It is the psychology also of modern civilized man, and not merely of individual 'throw backs' in modern society." I would go on to argue that, on the contrary, every civilized human being, however high his conscious development, is still an archaic man at the deeper levels of his psyche.

And, I submit, when you find that out—and solo backpacking is assuredly an excellent way to do so—your life will become much better, no matter what successes you have in the outer world. The archaic man feels that he has a bond, a participation mystique with all of nature—human nature or otherwise—a broad oneness, which I believe is the only path, the only trail to immortality. The body and mind will die, but the soul has no place and therefore cannot die—it lives on as a legacy for those not yet dead. Such immortal souls don't need a heaven or another world—those are just dreams, hopes for what cannot be. However, the archaic collective unconscious, when in imaginative dialogue with one's consciousness, gives one the sense of "immortality," which Thoreau had while metaphorically standing on the bank of a river and fishing for immortal archetypes of the soul, and Nietzsche had when he realized that the new immortality is that of *wishing* to live all of life again. This is not something that one can achieve through mere effort. Nietzsche's idea of the "eternal return" is not a metaphysical idea, but rather depth psychology. To wish all of life to "return"— the emphasis being on the *wish*—is to make all things "entangled, ensnared, enamored [...] *for all joy wants—eternity"*—Nietzsche, *Thus Spoke Zarathustra*, "The Drunken Song" (Dover Publications, 1999).

The archaic man apparently is driven by synchronicity, that connecting principle that pulls the inner and outer life together without causation, but rather by chance. The literal belief in spirits, ghosts, magicians, and fortune-tellers is not the archaic man's world, but rather the modern man's literalistic reading of ancient history. Archaic humans considered the realm of spirits to be mysterious forces that determine the outcomes of events for millennia, starting somewhere in the Paleolithic age. They used apotropaic magic and believed in shamanistic "mana," a more-than-ordinary human power. Their approach to nature fulfilled their lives—they did not seek to control nature but rather to survive within it, while learning about the human psyche… something that is still a mystery to modern humans.

Modern man (and I use the term "man" loosely and only in reflection of Jung's use of the word in the phrase "archaic man") lives for the control of externals; archaic man was more in control of his self, not separate from nature, but rather entirely one with nature. If we contemporary humans are to overcome what we call "nature deficit disorder," we must seek our inner "nature" and thus experience nature as our outward destiny.

Jung insisted in his *Archaic Man* that our "discovery of the unconscious means an enormous spiritual task, which must be accomplished if we wish to preserve our civilization."

And that meant:

> …civilized man […] is in danger of losing all contact with the world of instinct […] this loss of instinct is largely responsible for the pathological condition of contemporary culture […] As a matter of fact, primitive man is no more logical or illogical than we are. His presuppositions are not the same as ours, and that is what distinguishes him from us.

Archaic man presupposed that nature cannot be understood logically, since he had no science; whereas, because we know so much about nature, we have no need to turn inward and look at our souls. This "original man" (*archaic* can be defined as "original") did not need to control his world, and for him, chance was not an enemy or an "injustice." Like Nietzsche, he took life as it is, thereby considering life "all entangled, ensnared, enamored—for all joy wants eternity."

Can such a place as the Grand Canyon offer us the only eternity there is? That of human soulful experience? I had not expected as much when I decided to hike alone in solitude and silence. Yet that was the truth I found—spontaneous ecstasy.

To those who want to get closer to nature: such a "goal" cannot be achieved without participating in the inner journey. Everyone experiences the archaic inner journey as a child, but few of us realize it can be re-found in our unconscious and relived as a blessing in old age—a future "backpack" full of gratitude, wisdom, and joy.

I am not suggesting that in old age we should physically partake in solo backpacking: obviously, the dwindling strength in our bodies at some point makes carrying a large backpack impossible. But as we age, we should work on, and delight in, recalling our early ecstasy experiences, as I do in this book. *This* is why so many old people want to talk about the past.

Surely, joy is the condition of life.

BIBLIOGRAPHY

Abbey, Edward, *A Voice Crying in the Wilderness* (St. Martin's Griffin, 1989)

Annerino, John, *Hiking in the Grand Canyon* (Sierra Club Books, 1993)

Arnold, Matthew, *New Poems* (Macmillan and Co., 1867)

Barzun, Jacques, *From Dawn to Decadence 1500 to the Present* (Harper Collins, 2000)

Eliade, Mircea, *The Sacred and the Profane: The Nature of Religion* (Harcourt, Brace & World, 1959)

Eliade, Mircea *Shamanism: Archaic Techniques of Ecstasy* (Princeton University Press, 2004)

Euler, Robert and **Smithson, Carma Lee,** *Havasupai Legends: Religion and Mythology of the Havasupai in the Grand Canyon* (University of Utah Press, 2002)

Fletcher, Colin, *The Man Who Walked Through Time* (Alfred A. Knopf, 1967)

Fletcher, Colin, *The Secret Worlds of Colin Fletcher* (Knopf Doubleday, 1990)

Fletcher, Colin, *The Man from the Cave* (Vintage Books, 1982)

Freud, Sigmund, *Group Psychology and the Analysis of the Ego* (Bantam Books, 1960)

Ghiglieri, Michael and **Myers, Thomas,** *Over the Edge: Death in the Grand Canyon* (Puma Press, 2001)

Grey, Zane, *Tails of Lonely Trails* (Penguin Publishing Group, 1988)

Hillman, James, *The Force of Character* (Random House, 1999)

Hillman, James, *The Soul's Code* (Random House, 1996)

Jung, Carl, *Collected Works of Carl Jung, Vols. 2, 3, 8, and 12* (Princeton University Press, 1968)

Jung, Carl, *The Red Book* (W.W. Norton & Company, 2009)

Muir, John, *Steep Trails* (Vertebrate Publishing, 2018)

Nash, Roderick Frasier, *Wilderness and the American Mind* (Yale University Press, 4th Edition, 1982)

Neihardt, John, *Black Elk Speaks* (Excelsior Editions, 2008)

Nietzsche, Friedrich, *Beyond Good and Evil* (Penguin Publishing Group, 1990)

Nietzsche, Friedrich, *Genealogy of Morals* (Vintage: Reissue edition, 1989)

Nietzsche, Friedrich, *Thus Spoke Zarathustra, "The Drunken Song"* (Dover Publications, 1999)

Neumann, Mark, *On the Rim* (University of Minnesota Press, 2001)

Niehardt, John, *Black Elk Speaks* (Bison Books, 1972)

Noel, Daniel, *The Soul of Shamanism* (Continuum International Publishing Group, 1997)

Oelschlaeger, Max, *The Idea of Wilderness* (Yale University Press, 1991)

Phillips, Melanie, *The World Turned Upside Down: The Global Battle Over God, Truth, and Power* (Encounter Books, 2010)

Picard, Max, *The World of Silence* (Regnery Press, 1948)

Priestley, John Boynton, *Notes on an American Journey* (Harper's Magazine, 1935)

Ranney, Wayne, *Carving Grand Canyon: Evidence, Theories, and Mystery* (Grand Canyon Conservancy, 2012)

Rhodes, James, *Eros, Wisdom, and Silence: Plato's Erotic Dialogues* (University of Missouri Press, 2003)

Rusho, W.L., *Everett Ruess: A Vagabond for Beauty* (Peregrine Press, 1983)

Sabini, Meredith, *The Earth Has a Soul: C.G. Jung on Nature, Technology & Modern Life* (North Atlantic Books, 2002)

Schullery, Paul (editor), *The Grand Canyon Early Impressions* (Pruett Publishing Co., 1989)

Stegner, Wallace, *Mormon Country* (Duel, Sloan & Pearce, 1942)

Thomas, Dylan, *The Poems of Dylan Thomas* (New Directions; Annotated Edition, 2017)

Thoreau, Henry David, *The Journal of Thoreau, Vol. 2* (Peregrine Smith Books, 1984)

Thoreau, Henry David, *Walden* (Ticknor and Fields, 1854)

Thoreau, Henry David, *A Week on the Concord and Merrimack River* (Princeton University Press, 2004)

Thybony, Scott, *The Incredible Grand Canyon: Cliffhangers and Curiosities from America's Greatest Canyon* (Grand Canyon Association, 2007)

Warner, Charles Dudley, *Harper's Magazine* (1891)

White, William Allen, *McClure's Magazine* (1905)